JAMESTOWN EDUCATION

Timed Readings Plus
in Social Studies

BOOK 10

**25 Two-Part Lessons with Questions for
Building Reading Speed and Comprehension**

Mc Graw Hill **Glencoe**

New York, New York   Columbus, Ohio   Chicago, Illinois   Peoria, Illinois   Woodland Hills, California

JAMESTOWN EDUCATION

Glencoe

The *McGraw-Hill* Companies

ISBN: 0-07-845808-0

Send all queries to:
Glencoe/McGraw-Hill
8787 Orion Place
Columbus, OH 43240-4027

1 2 3 4 5 6 7 8 9 10 021 08 07 06 05 04 03

CONTENTS

TO THE STUDENT

You probably talk at an average rate of about 150 words a minute. If you are a reader of average ability, you read at a rate of about 250 words a minute. So your reading speed is nearly twice as fast as your speaking or listening speed. This example shows that reading is one of the fastest ways to get information.

The purpose of this book is to help you increase your reading rate and understand what you read. The 25 lessons in this book will also give you practice in reading social studies articles and in preparing for tests in which you must read and understand nonfiction passages within a certain time limit.

Reading Faster and Better

Following are some strategies that you can use to read the articles in each lesson.

Previewing

Previewing before you read is a very important step. This helps you to get an idea of what a selection is about and to recall any previous knowledge you have about the subject. Here are the steps to follow when previewing.

Read the title. Titles are designed not only to announce the subject but also to make the reader think. Ask yourself questions such as What can I learn from the title? What thoughts does it bring to mind?

What do I already know about this subject?

Read the first sentence. If they are short, read the first two sentences. The opening sentence is the writer's opportunity to get your attention. Some writers announce what they hope to tell you in the selection. Some writers state their purpose for writing; others just try to get your attention.

Read the last sentence. If it is short, read the final two sentences. The closing sentence is the writer's last chance to get ideas across to you. Some writers repeat the main idea once more. Some writers draw a conclusion—this is what they have been leading up to. Other writers summarize their thoughts; they tie all the facts together.

Skim the entire selection. Glance through the selection quickly to see what other information you can pick up. Look for anything that will help you read fluently and with under-standing. Are there names, dates, or numbers? If so, you may have to read more slowly.

Reading for Meaning

Here are some ways to make sure you are making sense of what you read.

Build your concentration. You cannot understand what you read if you are not concentrating. When you discover that your thoughts are straying, correct the situation right away. Avoid distractions and distracting situations. Keep in mind the information you learned from previewing. This will help focus your attention on the selection.

Read in thought groups. Try to see meaningful combinations of words—phrases, clauses, or sentences. If you look at only one word at a time (called word-by-word reading), both your comprehension and your reading speed suffer.

Ask yourself questions. To sustain the pace you have set for yourself and to maintain a high level of concentration and comprehension, ask yourself questions such as What does this mean? or How can I use this information? as you read.

Finding the Main Ideas

The paragraph is the basic unit of meaning. If you can quickly discover and understand the main idea of each paragraph, you will build your comprehension of the selection.

Find the topic sentence. The topic sentence, which contains the main idea, often is the first sentence of a paragraph. It is followed by sentences that support, develop, or explain the main idea. Sometimes a topic sentence comes at the end of a paragraph. When it does, the supporting details come first, building the base for the topic sentence. Some paragraphs do not have a topic sentence; all of the sentences combine to create a meaningful idea.

Understand paragraph structure. Every well-written paragraph has a purpose. The purpose may be to inform, define, explain, or illustrate. The purpose should always relate to the main idea and expand on it. As you read each paragraph, see how the body of the paragraph tells you more about the main idea.

Relate ideas as you read. As you read the selection, notice how the writer puts together ideas. As you discover the relationship between the ideas, the main ideas come through quickly and clearly.

Mastering Reading Comprehension

Reading fast is not useful if you don't remember or understand what you read. The two exercises in Part A provide a check on how well you have understood the article.

Recalling Facts

These multiple-choice questions provide a quick check to see how well you recall important information from the article. As you learn to apply the reading strategies described earlier, you should be able to answer these questions more successfully.

Understanding Ideas

These questions require you to think about the main ideas in the article. Some main ideas are stated in the article; others are not. To answer some of the questions, you need to draw conclusions about what you read.

The five exercises in Part B require multiple answers. These exercises provide practice in applying comprehension and critical thinking skills that you can use in all your reading.

Recognizing Words in Context

Always check to see whether the words around an unfamiliar word—its context—can give you a clue to the word's meaning. A word generally appears in a context related to its meaning.

Suppose, for example, that you are unsure of the meaning of the word *expired* in the following passage:

> Vera wanted to check out a book, but her library card had expired. She had to borrow my card, because she didn't have time to renew hers.

You could begin to figure out the meaning of *expired* by asking yourself a question such as, What could have happened to Vera's library card that would make her need to borrow someone else's card? You might realize that if Vera had to renew her card, its usefulness must have come to an end or run out. This would lead you to conclude that the word *expired* must mean "to come to an end" or "to run out." You would be right. The context suggested the meaning.

Context can also affect the meaning of a word you already know. The word *key,* for instance, has many meanings. There are musical keys, door keys, and keys to solving a mystery. The context in which the word *key* occurs will tell you which meaning is correct.

Sometimes a word is explained by the words that immediately follow it. The subject of a sentence and your knowledge about that subject might also help you determine the meaning of an unknown word. Try to decide the meaning of the word *revive* in the following sentence:

> Sunshine and water will revive those drooping plants.

The compound subject is *sunshine* and *water.* You know that plants need light and water to survive and that drooping plants are not healthy. You can figure out that *revive* means "to bring back to health."

Distinguishing Fact from Opinion

Every day you are called upon to sort out fact and opinion. Because much of what you read and hear contains both facts and opinions, you need to be able to tell the two apart.

Facts are statements that can be proved. The proof must be objective and verifiable. You must be able to check for yourself to confirm a fact.

Look at the following facts. Notice that they can be checked for accuracy and confirmed. Suggested sources for verification appear in parentheses.

- Abraham Lincoln was the 16th president of the United States. (Consult biographies, social studies books, encyclopedias, and similar sources.)

- Earth revolves around the Sun. (Research in encyclopedias or astronomy books; ask knowledgeable people.)

- Dogs walk on four legs. (See for yourself.)

Opinions are statements that cannot be proved. There is no objective evidence you can consult to check the truthfulness of an opinion. Unlike facts, opinions express personal beliefs or judgments. Opinions reveal how someone feels about a subject, not the facts about that subject. You might agree or disagree with someone's opinion, but you cannot prove it right or wrong.

Look at the following opinions. The reasons these statements are classified as opinions appear in parentheses.

- Abraham Lincoln was born to be a president. (You cannot prove this by referring to birth records. There is no evidence to support this belief.)

- Earth is the only planet in our solar system where intelligent life exists. (There is no proof of this. It may be proved true some day, but for now it is just an educated guess—not a fact.)

- The dog is a human's best friend. (This is not a fact; your best friend might not be a dog.)

As you read, be aware that facts and opinions are often mixed together. Both are useful to you as a reader. But to evaluate what you read and to read intelligently, you need to know the difference between the two.

Keeping Events in Order

Sequence, or chronological order, is the order of events in a story or article or the order of steps in a process. Paying attention to the sequence of events or steps will help you follow what is happening, predict what might happen next, and make sense of a passage.

To make the sequence as clear as possible, writers often use signal words to help the reader get a more exact idea of when things happen. Following is a list of frequently used signal words and phrases:

until	first
next	then
before	after
finally	later
when	while
during	now
at the end	by the time
as soon as	in the beginning

Signal words and phrases are also useful when a writer chooses to relate details or events out of sequence. You need to pay careful attention to determine the correct chronological order.

Making Correct Inferences

Much of what you read *suggests* more than it *says*. Writers often do not state ideas directly in a text. They can't. Think of the time and space it would take to state every idea. And think of how boring that would be! Instead, writers leave it to you, the reader, to fill in the information they leave out—to make inferences. You do this by combining clues in the story or article with knowledge from your own experience.

You make many inferences every day. Suppose, for example, that you are visiting a friend's house for the first time. You see a bag of kitty litter. You infer (make an inference) that the family has a cat. Another day you overhear a conversation. You catch the names of two actors and the words *scene, dialogue,* and *directing.* You infer that the people are discussing a movie or play.

In these situations and others like them, you infer unstated information from what you observe or read. Readers must make inferences in order to understand text.

Be careful about the inferences you make. One set of facts may suggest several inferences. Some of these inferences could be faulty. A correct inference must be supported by evidence.

Remember that bag of kitty litter that caused you to infer that your friend has a cat? That could be a faulty inference. Perhaps your friend's family uses the kitty litter on their icy sidewalks to create traction. To be sure your inference is correct, you need more evidence.

Understanding Main Ideas

The main idea is the most important idea in a paragraph or passage—the idea that provides purpose and direction. The rest of the selection explains, develops, or supports the main idea. Without a main idea, there would be only a collection of unconnected thoughts.

In the following paragraph, the main idea is printed in italics. As you read, observe how the other sentences develop or explain the main idea.

Typhoon Chris hit with full fury today on the central coast of Japan. Heavy rain from the storm flooded the area. High waves carried many homes into the sea. People now fear that the heavy rains will cause mudslides in the central part of the country. The number of people killed by the storm may climb past the 200 mark by Saturday.

In this paragraph, the main-idea statement appears first. It is followed by sentences that explain, support, or give details. Sometimes the main idea appears at the end of a paragraph. Writers often put the main idea at the end of a paragraph when their purpose is to persuade or convince. Readers may be more open to a new idea if the reasons for it are presented first.

As you read the following paragraph, think about the overall impact of the supporting ideas. Their purpose is to convince the reader that the main idea in the last sentence should be accepted.

Last week there was a head-on collision at Huntington and Canton streets. Just a month ago a pedestrian was struck there. Fortunately, she was only slightly injured. In the past year, there have been more accidents there than at any other corner in the city. In fact, nearly 10 percent of all accidents in the city occur at the corner. This intersection is very dangerous, and a traffic signal should be installed there before a life is lost.

The details in the paragraph progress from least important to most important. They achieve their full effect in the main idea statement at the end.

In many cases, the main idea is not expressed in a single sentence. The reader is called upon to interpret all of the ideas expressed in the paragraph and to decide upon a main idea. Read the following paragraph.

The American author Jack London was once a pupil at the Cole Grammar School in Oakland, California. Each morning the class sang a song. When the teacher noticed that Jack wouldn't sing, she sent him to the principal. He returned to class with a note. The note said that Jack could be excused from singing with the class if he would write an essay every morning.

In this paragraph, the reader has to interpret the individual ideas and to decide on a main idea. This main idea seems reasonable: Jack London's career as a writer began with a punishment in grammar school.

Understanding the concept of the main idea and knowing how to find it is important. Transferring that understanding to your reading and study is also important.

Working Through a Lesson

Part A

1. **Preview the article.** Locate the timed selection in Part A of the lesson that you are going to read. Wait for your teacher's signal to preview. You will have 20 seconds for previewing. Follow the previewing steps described on page 2.

2. **Read the article.** When your teacher gives you the signal, begin reading. Read carefully so that you will be able to answer questions about what you have read. When you finish reading, look at the board and note your reading time. Write this time at the bottom of the page on the line labeled Reading Time.

3. **Complete the exercises.** Answer the 10 questions that follow the article. There are 5 fact questions and 5 idea questions. Choose the best answer to each question and put an X in that box.

4. **Correct your work.** Use the Answer Key at the back of the book to check your answers. Circle any wrong answer and put an X in the box you should have marked. Record the number of correct answers on the appropriate line at the end of the lesson.

Part B

1. **Preview and read the passage.** Use the same techniques you

used to read Part A. Think about what you are reading.

2. **Complete the exercises.** Instructions are given for answering each category of question. There are 15 responses for you to record.

3. **Correct your work.** Use the Answer Key at the back of the book. Circle any wrong answer and write the correct letter or number next to it. Record the number of correct answers on the appropriate line at the end of the lesson.

Plotting Your Progress

1. **Find your reading rate.** Turn to the Reading Rate graph on page 116. Put an X at the point where the vertical line that represents the lesson intersects your reading time, shown along the left-hand side. The right-hand side of the graph will reveal your words-per-minute reading speed.

2. **Find your comprehension score.** Add your scores for Part A and Part B to determine your total number of correct answers. Turn to the Comprehension Score Graph on page 117. Put an X at the point where the vertical line that represents your lesson intersects your total correct answers, shown along the left-hand side. The right-hand side of the graph will show the percentage of questions you answered correctly.

3. **Complete the Comprehension Skills Profile.** Turn to page 118. Record your incorrect answers for the Part B exercises. The five Part B skills are listed along the bottom. There are five columns of boxes, one column for each question. For every incorrect answer, put an X in a box for that skill.

To get the most benefit from these lessons, you need to take charge of your own progress in improving your reading speed and comprehension. Studying these graphs will help you to see whether your reading rate is increasing and to determine what skills you need to work on. Your teacher will also review the graphs to check your progress.

TO THE TEACHER

About the Series

Timed Readings Plus in Social Studies includes 10 books at reading levels 4–13, with one book at each level. Book One contains material at a fourth-grade reading level; Book Two at a fifth-grade level, and so on. The readability level is determined by the Fry Readability Scale and is not to be confused with grade or age level of the student. The books are designed for use with students at middle school level and above.

The purposes of the series are as follows:

- to provide systematic, structured reading practice that helps students improve their reading rate and comprehension skills

- to give students practice in reading and understanding informational articles in the content area of social studies

- to give students experience in reading various text types—informational, expository, narrative, and prescriptive

- to prepare students for taking standardized tests that include timed reading passages in various content areas

- to provide materials with a wide range of reading levels so that students can continue to practice and improve their reading rate and comprehension skills

Because the books are designed for use with students at designated reading levels rather than in a particular grade, the social studies topics in this series are not correlated to any grade-level curriculum. Most standardized tests require students to read and comprehend social studies passages. This series provides an opportunity for students to become familiar with the particular requirements of reading social studies. For example, the vocabulary in a social studies article is important. Students need to know certain words in order to understand the concepts and the information.

Each book in the series contains 25 two-part lessons. Part A focuses on improving reading rate. This section of the lesson consists of a 400-word timed informational article on a social studies topic followed by two multiple-choice exercises. Recalling Facts includes five fact questions; Understanding Ideas includes five critical thinking questions.

Part B concentrates on building mastery in critical areas of comprehension. This section consists of a nontimed passage—the "plus" passage—followed by five exercises that address five major comprehension skills. The passage varies in length; its subject matter relates to the content of the timed selection.

Timed Reading and Comprehension

Timed reading is the best-known method of improving reading speed. There is no point in someone's reading at an accelerated speed if the person does not understand what she or he is reading. Nothing is more important than comprehension in reading. The main purpose of reading is to gain knowledge and insight, to understand the information that the writer and the text are communicating.

Few students will be able to read a passage once and answer all of the questions correctly. A score of 70 or 80 percent correct is normal. If the student gets 90 or 100 percent correct, he or she is either reading too slowly or the material is at too low a reading level. A comprehension or critical thinking score of less than 70 percent indicates a need for improvement.

One method of improving comprehension and critical thinking skills is for the student to go back and study each incorrect answer. First, the student should reread the question carefully. It is surprising how many students get the wrong answer simply because they have not read the question carefully. Then the student should look back in the passage to find the place where the question is answered, reread that part of the passage, and think about how to arrive at the correct answer. It is important to be able to recognize a correct answer when it

is embedded in the text. Teacher guidance or class discussion will help the student find an answer.

Speed Versus Comprehension

It is not unusual for comprehension scores to decline as reading rate increases during the early weeks of timed readings. If this happens, students should attempt to level off their speed—but not lower it—and concentrate more on comprehension. Usually, if students maintain the higher speed and concentrate on comprehension, scores will gradually improve and within a week or two be back up to normal levels of 70 to 80 percent.

It is important to achieve a proper balance between speed and comprehension. An inefficient reader typically reads everything at one speed, usually slowly. Some poor readers, however, read rapidly but without satisfactory comprehension. It is important to achieve a balance between speed and comprehension. The practice that this series provides enables students to increase their reading speed while maintaining normal levels of comprehension.

Getting Started

As a rule, the passages in a book designed to improve reading speed should be relatively easy. The student should not have much difficulty with the vocabulary or the subject matter. Don't worry about the passages being too easy; students should see how quickly and efficiently they can read a passage.

Begin by assigning students to a level. A student should start with a book that is one level below his or her current reading level. If a student's reading level is not known, a suitable starting point would be one or two levels below the student's present grade in school.

Introduce students to the contents and format of the book they are using. Examine the book to see how it is organized. Talk about the parts of each lesson. Discuss the purpose of timed reading and the use of the progress graphs at the back of the book.

Timing the Reading

One suggestion for timing the reading is to have all students begin reading the selection at the same time. After one minute, write on the board the time that has elapsed and begin updating it at 10-second intervals (1:00, 1:10, 1:20, etc.). Another option is to have individual students time themselves with a stopwatch.

Teaching a Lesson

Part A

1. Give students the signal to begin previewing the lesson. Allow 20 seconds, then discuss special terms or vocabulary that students found.

2. Use one of the methods described above to time students as they read the passage. (Include the 20-second preview time as part of the first minute.) Tell students to write down the last time shown on the board or the stopwatch when they finish reading. Have them record the time in the designated space after the passage.

3. Next, have students complete the exercises in Part A. Work with them to check their answers, using the Answer Key that begins on page 114. Have them circle incorrect answers, mark the correct answers, and then record the numbers of correct answers for Part A on the appropriate line at the end of the lesson. Correct responses to eight or more questions indicate satisfactory comprehension and recall.

Part B

1. Have students read the Part B passage and complete the exercises that follow it. Directions are provided with each exercise. Correct responses require deliberation and discrimination.

2. Work with students to check their answers. Then discuss the answers with them and have them record the number of correct answers for Part B at the end of the lesson.

Have students study the correct answers to the questions they answered incorrectly. It is important that they understand why a particular answer is correct or incorrect.

Have them reread relevant parts of a passage to clarify an answer. An effective cooperative activity is to have students work in pairs to discuss their answers, explain why they chose the answers they did, and try to resolve differences.

Monitoring Progress

Have students find their total correct answers for the lesson and record their reading time and scores on the graphs on pages 116 and 117. Then have them complete the Comprehension Skills Profile on page 118. For each incorrect response to a question in Part B, students should mark an X in the box above each question type.

The legend on the Reading Rate graph automatically converts reading times to words-per-minute rates. The Comprehension Score graph automatically converts the raw scores to percentages.

These graphs provide a visual record of a student's progress. This record gives the student and you an opportunity to evaluate the student's progress and to determine the types of exercises and skills he or she needs to concentrate on.

Diagnosis and Evaluation

The following are typical reading rates.

Slow Reader—150 Words Per Minute

Average Reader—250 Words Per Minute

Fast Reader—350 Words Per Minute

A student who consistently reads at an average or above-average rate (with satisfactory comprehension) is ready to advance to the next book in the series.

A column of Xs in the Comprehension Skills Profile indicates a specific comprehension weakness. Using the profile, you can assess trends in student performance and suggest remedial work if necessary.

The Oregon Trail

Before the middle of the nineteenth century, only a handful of Americans had crossed the continent of North America overland. The earliest settlers from the East often arrived by boat after a yearlong voyage that took them south into the Antarctic waters, around the tip of South America, and then back north again. The Oregon Trail, by contrast, made it possible for people from the East to reach the territories along the Pacific Coast in only four to six months. In 1842 Dr. Elijah White led the first wagon train to Oregon, and by 1843 the trickle of emigrants heading west became a river as more than 1,000 people made the trip. After the discovery of gold in California in 1849, the river became a flood, and wagon wheels carved so deeply into the ground that in places ruts are still visible today.

The Oregon Trail began in Independence, Missouri, on the Missouri River, and covered about 2,000 miles of prairies, mountains, and deserts. Long, circuitous, and difficult, it took advantage of the routes established by Native Americans and European fur trappers, which meandered around the region. Portions of it were mapped during the Lewis and Clark Expedition (1804–1806). Later, a number of businessmen financed the creation of trading posts along the way. The trail was also used by the Army, stagecoaches carrying passengers from town to town, and even Pony Express riders who were carrying the mail.

The long trip on the Oregon Trail was very dangerous. One person in 10 died along the way—some from hunger, disease, or accidents, and others in storms or by drowning. Families needed to carry about 1,000 pounds of nonperishable foods (such as flour and bacon, salt, sugar, and coffee) in wagons drawn by oxen or mules. They also carried water barrels, guns, ammunition, and tools, which left very little space for bedding, clothes, books, and household items—or for the pioneers themselves. Everyone who could walk did so. Many pioneers walked most of the 2,000 miles. Native Americans, many of whom were initially helpful to the travelers, later became hostile as they watched their homelands being overrun by these strangers.

As the network of fast and comfortable railroads connecting American cities expanded westward, traffic on the Oregon Trail declined. The completion of the transcontinental railroad in 1869 ended the Oregon Trail's dominance as the primary route to the West.

Reading Time _____

Recalling Facts

1. Crossing the Oregon Trail took most people between
   - ❏ a. 1 and 2 years.
   - ❏ b. 6 months and 1 year.
   - ❏ c. 4 and 6 months.

2. The Oregon Trail began in
   - ❏ a. Missouri.
   - ❏ b. Massachusetts.
   - ❏ c. Nebraska.

3. Foods commonly packed for the journey included
   - ❏ a. flour, milk and bacon.
   - ❏ b. coffee, bacon, and sugar.
   - ❏ c. bacon, eggs, and bread.

4. The primary reason behind the decline in the importance of the Oregon Trail was
   - ❏ a. the expansion of the railroads.
   - ❏ b. a traveler's preference for sea travel.
   - ❏ c. a lack of interest in traveling west.

5. One of the signs left today that suggests that the Oregon Trail was heavily traveled is
   - ❏ a. the pavement laid by the pioneers.
   - ❏ b. wheel ruts visible in the ground.
   - ❏ c. articles of clothing left behind by the settlers.

Understanding Ideas

6. One can conclude from this passage that the Oregon Trail was the primary route west for
   - ❏ a. about 150 years.
   - ❏ b. about 100 years.
   - ❏ c. about 25 years.

7. One can conclude from the context that a circuitous route
   - ❏ a. is straight and direct.
   - ❏ b. often winds back and forth.
   - ❏ c. is sparsely traveled.

8. This passage suggests that the Oregon Trail
   - ❏ a. was made famous by the Lewis and Clark expedition.
   - ❏ b. was laid out by the gold miners.
   - ❏ c. is made up of many shorter trails.

9. Which of the following is a reasonable inference from this passage?
   - ❏ a. There were great risks for people traveling on the Oregon Trail.
   - ❏ b. Crossing rivers was the most dangerous aspect of the trip.
   - ❏ c. Doctors often accompanied travelers during the journey west.

10. One can conclude from the passage that
    - ❏ a. it was less expensive to travel to Oregon by rail than by wagon train.
    - ❏ b. it was more comfortable to travel to Oregon by wagon train than by rail.
    - ❏ c. speed of travel determined the preferred means of transportation.

14

The Prairie Schooner

People traveled west, using wagons, along the Oregon Trail. However, 2,000 rigorous miles were more challenging than most wagons could manage. The massive Conestoga wagons, popular in the East for hauling freight since the eighteenth century, were too unwieldy to negotiate high mountain passes and treacherous river crossings. Some travelers started out with their possessions in a wheelbarrow or handcart, and many families, of course, made the trip in ordinary farm carts retrofitted with canvas coverings.

The wagon emblematic of the Oregon Trail, however, was the Prairie Schooner. Patterned after the Conestoga wagon, but half its size to be managed easily, it was typically powered by teams of four to six oxen or six to ten mules.

A complex undercarriage mechanism made the Prairie Schooner a flexible wagon that could negotiate sharp turns. It also had a deep wagon bed that could be made watertight with a coat of tar and floated like a boat across rivers. The canvas bonnet extended slightly past the ends of the wagon bed for additional protection; this bonnet could be drawn tight to keep out the dust and treated with linseed oil to shed the rain better.

Although the Prairie Schooner was well designed and durable, it still broke down frequently, and travelers kept tools and materials needed to make repairs in a large box attached to the side of the wagon.

1. **Recognizing Words in Context**

   Find the word *emblematic* in the passage. One definition below is closest to the meaning of that word. One definition has the opposite or nearly the opposite meaning. The remaining definition has a completely different meaning. Label the definitions C for *closest,* O for *opposite or nearly opposite,* and D for *different.*

   _____ a. not representative

   _____ b. symbolic

   _____ c. undeserving

2. **Distinguishing Fact from Opinion**

   Two of the statements below present *facts,* which can be proved. The other statement is an *opinion,* which expresses someone's thoughts or beliefs. Label the statements F for *fact* and O for *opinion.*

   _____ a. The size of Conestoga wagons were a problem on the Oregon Trail.

   _____ b. Usually, mule teams or oxen pulled the Prairie Schooners.

   _____ c. The Prairie Schooner was the best-designed wagon that was ever built.

3. Keeping Events in Order

Two of the statements below describe events that took place at the same time. The other statement describes an event that took place before or after those events. Label them S for *same time*, B for *before*, and A for *after*.

_____ a. Some families traveling west fit their farm wagons with a canvas cover for protection.

_____ b. the Conestoga Wagon is developed to haul heavy freight.

_____ c The Prairie Schooner becomes popular with travelers headed out on the Oregon Trail.

4. Making Correct Inferences

Two of the statements below are correct *inferences,* or reasonable guesses. They are based on information in the passage. The other statement is an incorrect, or faulty, inference. Label the statements C for *correct* inference and F for *faulty* inference.

_____ a. Travelers were likely to encounter extreme variations in weather along the Oregon Trail.

_____ b. Farm carts retrofitted with canvas coverings were as efficient as the Prairie Schooner.

_____ c. Most travelers along the Oregon Trail were self-sufficient and able to solve many kinds of problems.

5. Understanding Main Ideas

One of the statements below expresses the main idea of the passage. One statement is too general, or too broad. The other explains only part of the passage; it is too narrow. Label the statements M for *main idea*, B for *too broad*, and N for *too narrow*.

_____ a. Various types of wagons were used for various purposes in America.

_____ b. The Prairie Schooner was among the most popular and best-designed wagons on the Oregon Trail.

_____ c. The Prairie Schooner was patterned after the Conestoga wagon but was only half the size.

Correct Answers, Part A _____

Correct Answers, Part B _____

Total Correct Answers _____

16

Culture: A Total Identity

The term *culture* now is used to describe everything from the fine arts to the outlook of a business group or a sports team. In its original sense, however, *culture* embraces all identifying aspects of an ethnic group, nation, or empire: its physical environment, history, and traditions; its social rules and economic structure; its religious beliefs and arts.

The central beliefs and customs of a group are handed down from one generation to another. It is for this reason that most people regard culture as learned rather than innate. People acquire a culture; they are not born with one. The process by which a person develops a taste for regional foods, accented speech, or an outlook on the world over time, therefore, is known as *enculturation*.

Cultures are often identified by their symbols—images that are familiar and layered with meaning. Totem poles carved with animal and creative figures evoke aspects of the Native American peoples of the Pacific Northwest but more literally represent specific clans or families. In Asia and India, the color of saffron yellow is identified with Buddhist and Hindu priests; in ancient China it was a color only the emperor's family was allowed to wear. Thus, different cultures may respond to a symbol quite differently. For example, to some a flag may represent pride, historical accomplishments, or ideals; to others, however, it can mean danger or oppression.

To individuals unfamiliar with cultures outside their own, the beliefs, behaviors, and artistic expression of other groups can seem strange and even threatening. A society that ranks all other cultures against its own standards is said to be *ethnocentric* (from the Greek *ethnos,* meaning "tribe" or "people," and *kentros,* meaning "center"). A strongly ethnocentric society assumes also that what is different from its own culture is likely to be inferior and, possibly, wrong or evil.

All people are ethnocentric to some degree, and aspects of ethnocentrism, such as national pride, contribute to a well-functioning society. An appreciation for one's own culture, however, does not preclude acceptance and respect for another culture. History documents the long-term vigor and success of multicultural groups in which people from numerous and diverse cultural backgrounds live and work together. Ethnocentrism, in contrast, can lead to racism—the belief that it is race and ethnic origin that account for variations in human character or ability and that one's own race is inherently superior to all others.

Reading Time _____

Recalling Facts

1. The definition that most accurately describes culture today is
   - ❑ a. the literature, music, and painting of a nation.
   - ❑ b. all aspects of an ethnic group, nation, or empire.
   - ❑ c. the language and celebrations of a nation.

2. The central beliefs and customs of a culture
   - ❑ a. are based solely on the economy of a nation.
   - ❑ b. typically undergo great change every 50 years.
   - ❑ c. are handed down from one generation to the next.

3. Culture is generally regarded as _____ rather than _____
   - ❑ a. learned, innate.
   - ❑ b. natural, learned.
   - ❑ c. ethnocentric, patriotic.

4. A society that evaluates other cultures against its own standards is said to be
   - ❑ a. enculturated.
   - ❑ b. multicultural.
   - ❑ c. ethnocentric.

5. The term *ethnocentrism* derives in part from the Greek word meaning
   - ❑ a. culture.
   - ❑ b. tribe.
   - ❑ c. superiority.

Understanding Ideas

6. One can infer from this passage that
   - ❑ a. there is probably no aspect of a society that is not a part of its culture.
   - ❑ b. culture is unaffected by geography and climate.
   - ❑ c. members of the same culture get along easily with one another.

7. Which of the following is likely to be more of an innate characteristic than a learned one?
   - ❑ a. respect
   - ❑ b. shyness
   - ❑ c. patriotism

8. According to this passage, a symbol
   - ❑ a. is understood universally.
   - ❑ b. carries little meaning beyond its own culture.
   - ❑ c. may inspire different and opposing emotions.

9. One can infer from this passage that culture
   - ❑ a. does not affect individual identity.
   - ❑ b. is superficial.
   - ❑ c. is very much part of an individual's identity.

10. One can conclude from this passage that respect and acceptance of different cultures is
    - ❑ a. typical of an enthnocentric society.
    - ❑ b. itself a cultural attitude.
    - ❑ c. an innate ability.

What Is Cultural Anthropology?

Anthropology is the study of the origin of human groups and of their customs and traditions. Cultural anthropology considers human relations in groups. As the science has advanced, scientists' attitudes toward the nature and meaning of culture have changed.

At the end of the nineteenth century, Lewis Henry Morgan believed that human societies passed through three stages: in the "savage" stage were those in a basic hunter-gatherer culture; in the "barbaric" stage were preliterate groups starting to grow food and tame animals; in the "civilized" stage were those beginning to write. Any group that lacked a written language, he concluded, could not have a culture. Such a group had to be less intelligent than literate groups.

In the early twentieth century, Franz Boas separated the idea of culture from that of technical skill, arguing that differences in the achievements of societies resulted from past events and social and geographic conditions, not from innate intelligence. He also said that all cultures were complete, fully developed, and equally important.

Ethnologists today study social groups and cultures in order to understand each on its own terms. Their studies of the aboriginal cultures of Australia and South America, the nomadic peoples of Asia, and even the hip-hop youth culture in cities offer new insights into human beings.

1. **Recognizing Words in Context**

   Find the word *literate* in the passage. One definition below is closest to the meaning of that word. One definition has the opposite or nearly the opposite meaning. The remaining definition has a completely different meaning. Label the definitions C for *closest*, O for *opposite or nearly opposite*, and D for *different*.

   _____ a. popular

   _____ b. educated

   _____ c. ignorant

2. **Distinguishing Fact from Opinion**

   Two of the statements below present *facts*, which can be proved. The other statement is an *opinion*, which expresses someone's thoughts or beliefs. Label the statements F for *fact* and O for *opinion*.

   _____ a. Over the years, scientists have changed their views on the nature of culture.

   _____ b. All societies have fully developed and equally valuable cultures.

   _____ c. Anthropology is the study of human beings.

3. Keeping Events in Order

Number the statements below 1, 2, and 3 to show the order in which the events took place.

_____ a. Cultural anthropologists tried to understand each group they studied on its own terms.

_____ b. One school of thought believed that societies acquire culture as they move from a "savage" state to a "civilized" state.

_____ c. Franz Boas asserted that any society, whether advanced or not advanced technologically, has a fully developed culture.

4. Making Correct Inferences

Two of the statements below are correct *inferences*, or reasonable guesses. They are based on information in the passage. The other statement is an incorrect, or faulty, inference. Label the statements C for *correct* inference and F for *faulty* inference.

_____ a. Today cultural anthropologists might study female cadets and the military culture at West Point.

_____ b. Today cultural anthropologists strive for objectivity when recording their observations.

_____ c. Today cultural anthropologists are primarily interested in cultures in remote areas of the earth.

5. Understanding Main Ideas

One of the statements below expresses the main idea of the passage. One statement is too general, or too broad. The other explains only part of the passage; it is too narrow. Label the statements M for *main idea*, B for *too broad*, and N for *too narrow*.

_____ a. In cultural anthropology, theories about the nature of society and culture have changed over time.

_____ b. Cultural anthropology is a major area of study in the social sciences.

_____ c. Cultural anthropologists have studied hip-hop cultures in cities.

Correct Answers, Part A _____

Correct Answers, Part B _____

Total Correct Answers _____

The Military and Careers in Aviation

Aviation is much more than flying an airplane; it is a whole field of careers in computer and mechanical sciences, communications, education, law, medicine, and management. Aviation in the U.S. Armed Services takes place on land and at sea as well as in the air. In the Army, for example, 26 of 212 jobs touch on aviation in some way. These jobs exist in the areas of field artillery, electronic maintenance and certification, aircraft maintenance, and aviation operations.

Avionics is a key specialty; it focuses on flight-control systems. The word is derived from the old phrase "aviation electronics." In avionics one might design, build, or maintain the electronic instruments used in flight. These instruments permit communications between aircraft and with the ground, and they control steering, speed, altitude, and even the deployment of an aircraft's weapons. Air traffic-control systems also depend on avionics. These systems track and coordinate the movements of aircraft as they take off and land.

Some aviation jobs in the Armed Services require skills such as medical training. The U.S. Coast Guard, for instance, is dedicated to the patrol and safety of American waters. Rescue crews may have to fly through storms and around obstacles, jump into raging seas, transfer victims to helicopters or ships, and administer first aid. Such work is both physically demanding and extremely dangerous.

Pilots in today's military service operate every kind of aircraft there is, including small helicopters, gigantic transport planes, fighter jets, and the space shuttle. Military pilots hold the rank of officer and are both well educated and highly trained. In the Navy, future pilots must have earned a bachelor's degree before they may attend Aviation Officer Candidate School. Their basic flight and navigation training includes academic study and physical-fitness training as well as flying lessons. The next phases of training are designed to improve their skills and prepare them for specific missions.

For some eager pilots, the sky will never be the limit. Many of these aficionados of flight see the military as the direct road to outer space, as astronauts; but not all astronauts are pilots, of course. Mission and payload specialists are responsible for equipment maintenance, care of the astronauts' health and needs, and scientific research conducted in space. Pilot astronauts must have a bachelor's degree in engineering, mathematics, or a related field, and a minimum of 1,000 hours flying jet aircraft.

Reading Time _____

Recalling Facts

1. The field of aviation
   - ❏ a. focuses on the skills needed by a pilot.
   - ❏ b. requires a bachelor's degree in engineering, mathematics, or a related field.
   - ❏ c. includes careers in such fields as the mechanical sciences, communications, and medicine.

2. The area of avionics focuses on
   - ❏ a. flight-control systems.
   - ❏ b. flight-related health issues.
   - ❏ c. the design of jet engines.

3. The U.S. Coast Guard is dedicated to the safety and patrol of American waters and
   - ❏ a. uses only ships and other watercraft for its missions.
   - ❏ b. uses aviation for some rescue work.
   - ❏ c. does not engage in life-threatening work as other branches of the military do.

4. Pilots in today's military service
   - ❏ a. are generally assigned to aircraft used in battle.
   - ❏ b. fly aircraft of every description.
   - ❏ c. often go to flight school directly from high school.

5. To qualify for the astronaut pilot program, one must
   - ❏ a. be an officer in the military.
   - ❏ b. have at least a bachelor's degree and a minimum of 1,000 hours flying jet aircraft.
   - ❏ c. be able to fly all kinds of aircraft.

Understanding Ideas

6. One can conclude from the passage that the field of aviation
   - ❏ a. requires an advanced education in science and mathematics.
   - ❏ b. offers a range of opportunities for people with varying skills and interests.
   - ❏ c. is under the control of the U.S. Armed Services.

7. According to this passage, it seems likely that a typical military pilot must
   - ❏ a. demonstrate that he or she is physically fit.
   - ❏ b. be skilled at working mechanical and electronic devices.
   - ❏ c. have medical training.

8. An individual interested in becoming a military pilot should
   - ❏ a. probably begin by taking flying lessons.
   - ❏ b. have a strong interest in flying to outer space.
   - ❏ c. concentrate on science and technology subjects in school.

9. It seems likely that a person with an interest in avionics
   - ❏ a. would be unlikely to advance far in the military.
   - ❏ b. would find many opportunities in the space program.
   - ❏ c. would enlist in the Army rather than the Coast Guard.

10. A synonym for the word *aficionado* might be
    - ❏ a. opponent.
    - ❏ b. educator.
    - ❏ c. enthusiast.

Aircraft Carriers: A Nation Afloat

An aircraft carrier is an enormous warship, a veritable airfield in the middle of an ocean. The first aircraft carrier—the Kitty Hawk—went into service in 1961. Since then, three more classes of carriers have improved on the original design, integrating new technology and changing to meet the military needs of the age. The most modern of these behemoths is the nuclear-powered *Nimitz*-class carrier. The next class of carrier, the CVNX-1 design, is likely to go into service some time about 2013.

Nicknamed a "flattop" because of the expansive flight deck built above the larger hangar deck, a *Nimitz*-class carrier can accommodate more than 6,000 people and 85 aircraft. Because a tour of duty for the troops may last six months, almost every activity imaginable is carried out onboard. Meals are served around the clock; and entertainment, education, and health and business services are as much a part of life as military duties.

The carrier mission is tripartite. The deployment of carriers around the globe is intended to provide a significant military presence. The carriers serve to deter hostile actions on the part of various countries, they become a center of operations that serves United States forces and allies, and they provide a base from which the United States can protect its own forces and other friendly military forces and can launch attacks.

1. **Recognizing Words in Context**

   Find the word *behemoths* in the passage. One definition below is closest to the meaning of that word. One definition has the opposite or nearly the opposite meaning. The remaining definition has a completely different meaning. Label the definitions C for *closest*, O for *opposite or nearly opposite*, and D for *different*.

   _____ a. giants

   _____ b miniatures

   _____ c. yachts

2. **Distinguishing Fact from Opinion**

   Two of the statements below present *facts*, which can be proved. The other statement is an *opinion*, which expresses someone's thoughts or beliefs. Label the statements F for *fact* and O for *opinion*.

   _____ a. The presence of aircraft carriers in international waters is the best deterrent to hostile actions.

   _____ b. In times of crisis, American and allied forces can use the carrier as a base.

   _____ c. A *Nimitz*-class carrier can accommodate more than 6,000 people.

3. Keeping Events in Order

Number the statements below 1, 2, and 3 to show the order in which the events took place.

_____ a. The aircraft carrier Kitty Hawk goes into service.

_____ b The CVNX-1 design is planned to go into service.

_____ c. Nuclear power is used to drive the *Nimitz*-class carriers.

4. Making Correct Inferences

Two of the statements below are correct *inferences,* or reasonable guesses. They are based on information in the passage. The other statement is an incorrect, or faulty, inference. Label the statements C for *correct* inference and F for *faulty* inference.

_____ a. Life on an aircraft carrier is similar to that on a luxury cruise ship.

_____ b. New carrier designs reflect the needs of the military over the course of time.

_____ c. It takes a long time to design and build each aircraft carrier.

5. Understanding Main Ideas

One of the statements below expresses the main idea of the passage. One statement is too general, or too broad. The other explains only part of the passage; it is too narrow. Label the statements M for *main idea*, B for *too broad*, and N for *too narrow*.

_____ a. Nuclear-powered *Nimitz*-class aircraft carriers are the most modern carriers in service

_____ b. Aircraft carriers are part of an overall strategic military plan.

_____ c. Aircraft carriers are mobile military bases that are intended to keep peace and protect the United States and its allies.

Correct Answers, Part A _____

Correct Answers, Part B _____

Total Correct Answers _____

Honduras and Hurricane Mitch

In 1998 Hurricane Mitch, the deadliest Atlantic hurricane since 1780, took a devastating toll on Central America. Among the countries hardest hit was Honduras. Mitch's fury battered the area from October 26 to November 4, generating sustained winds of 155 miles per hour and gusts reaching well beyond 200 miles per hour. As the storm moved slowly westward across Honduras, it picked up moisture from both the Caribbean Sea and the Pacific Ocean. Up to two feet of rain per day fell in the mountains, creating floods and mudslides that swept away entire villages.

Honduras was once part of the far-reaching Maya civilization. Its indigenous populations declined precipitously after Spain colonized the country in the sixteenth century. On the north, Honduras meets the Caribbean Sea along a 400-mile coastline. Its interior is a landscape of fertile plains broken up by deep valleys and high mountains. Honduran natural resources include forests and mineral deposits. The clear-cutting of trees to make a profit and to create farmlands—as well as aggressive mining for silver and zinc—has left the land exposed to erosion. Rivers and lakes have been polluted by chemical runoff. Honduras is a relatively poor country with a turbulent political history: even before Hurricane Mitch, it had long battled such problems as malnutrition, disease, and poor housing. These factors heightened Honduras's vulnerablity to Mitch's attack.

Although exact numbers were never determined with total certainty, the final death toll from the hurricane exceeded 11,000. Three million Hondurans were severely affected or left homeless, prompting Honduran President Carlos Flores Facusse to describe the damage as the destruction of 50 years of progress. Whole villages were washed away. Also, perhaps 75 percent of the country's transportation infrastructure—including most of its bridges and secondary roads—was destroyed. Mitch also ruined most of Honduras's valuable export crops of coffee and bananas. The financial cost of the storm was set at more than five billion American dollars.

Recovery from this disaster is ongoing and time consuming. Problems include epidemics of diseases carried by foul water and sewage, food short-ages, and the influx of millions of people—who come in search of food, shelter, and work—from the country to the cities.

Among the countries providing disaster assistance are the United States, Mexico, Spain, Canada, and Japan. Two former U.S. presidents, George H. W. Bush and Jimmy Carter, visited Central America after the storm.

Reading Time _____

Recalling Facts

1. Hurricane Mitch, in 1998, was the deadliest Atlantic hurricane since
   - ❑ a. 1780.
   - ❑ b. 1980.
   - ❑ c. 1920.

2. During that storm, Honduras experienced
   - ❑ a. limited amounts of rain.
   - ❑ b. a number of earthquakes.
   - ❑ c. floods and mudslides.

3. Honduras's coastline extends hundreds of miles along the
   - ❑ a. Pacific Ocean.
   - ❑ b. Caribbean Sea.
   - ❑ c. Gulf of Mexico.

4. About _____ of Honduras's transportation infrastructure was destroyed by Hurricane Mitch.
   - ❑ a. 75 percent
   - ❑ b. 50 percent
   - ❑ c. 25 percent

5. Which of the following is *not* mentioned in this passage as a source of income for Honduras?
   - ❑ a. Coffee and bananas
   - ❑ b. Rubber
   - ❑ c. Silver

Understanding Ideas

6. One can infer that a hurricane
   - ❑ a. always moves more rapidly when it has strong winds.
   - ❑ b. is most dangerous in mountain areas.
   - ❑ c. can have high winds and still move slowly.

7. From the passage, one might infer that an abundance of natural resources in Honduras has
   - ❑ a. not resulted in prosperity for many of its citizens.
   - ❑ b. formed a strong economy.
   - ❑ c. helped Honduras recover quickly from Hurricane Mitch.

8. One might infer that
   - ❑ a. transportation in Honduras before Hurricane Mitch was modern and efficient.
   - ❑ b. the bulk of the transportation infrastructure in Honduras was developed before 1900.
   - ❑ c. most of the bridges and roads were built since the 1940s.

9. One could infer that the damage caused by Hurricane Mitch
   - ❑ a. received only local attention.
   - ❑ b. was addressed mostly by the countries of Central America.
   - ❑ c. was a concern around the world.

10. Which of the following sentences best represents the main idea?
   - ❑ a. Hurricane Mitch caused a tremendous amount of destruction in Honduras in 1998.
   - ❑ b. Recovery from the hurricane has been time consuming.
   - ❑ c. Hurricanes can cause devastating losses.

The United Nations and Disaster Relief

In the event of a crisis anywhere in the world, a host of private and public groups spring into action. None of them has a longer reach, however, than the Office for the Coordination of Humanitarian Affairs (OCHA), which is an arm of the United Nations (UN).

The UN, established in 1945, is based in New York City. Most people know it as a political body that works for world peace, but it is also concerned with such issues as health care, education, and economic development. Although the UN is relatively new, its work follows closely that of the 1899 International Peace Conference and the League of Nations founded in 1919. In 1992 the UN formed OCHA to focus on the civilian victims of conflicts and natural disasters.

OCHA directs donations and aid from around the world to crises both natural and caused by human actions. The organization launches appeals for assistance and also manages activities in the affected region and monitors the progress of relief efforts.

OCHA supports the creation of policies to deal with ongoing and potential problems, and it works to bring attention to issues that "fall between the cracks" and do not receive notice from other groups.

In addition, OCHA is a tireless advocate for disenfranchised people, such as minority groups, the homeless, and refugees.

1. **Recognizing Words in Context**

   Find the word *disenfranchised* in the passage. One definition below is closest to the meaning of that word. One definition has the opposite or nearly the opposite meaning. The remaining definition has a completely different meaning. Label the definitions C for *closest*, O for *opposite or nearly opposite*, and D for *different*.

   _____ a. influential

   _____ b. mesmerized

   _____ c. powerless

2. **Distinguishing Fact from Opinion**

   Two of the statements below present *facts*, which can be proved. The other statement is an *opinion*, which expresses someone's thoughts or beliefs. Label the statements F for *fact* and O for *opinion*.

   _____ a. The goals of the UN were pursued even before the organization was founded.

   _____ b. The UN is one of many organizations prepared to assist the victims of natural disasters.

   _____ c. The UN is effective in its promotion of world peace.

3. Keeping Events in Order

Number the statements below 1, 2, and 3 to show the order in which the events took place.

_____ a. The United Nations is formally established.

_____ b. The League of Nations carries on some of the work begun by the International Peace Conference.

_____ c. OCHA helps the victims of conflicts and natural disasters.

4. Making Correct Inferences

Two of the statements below are correct *inferences,* or reasonable guesses. They are based on information in the passage. The other statement is an incorrect, or faulty, inference. Label the statements C for *correct* inference and F for *faulty* inference.

_____ a. In the event of a natural disaster, all organizations work through OCHA to provide assistance.

_____ b. The building of schools and health clinics is an interest of the UN.

_____ c. OCHA focuses part of its resources on preparing for situations that are likely to occur in the future.

5. Understanding Main Ideas

One of the statements below expresses the main idea of the passage. One statement is too general, or too broad. The other explains only part of the passage; it is too narrow. Label the statements M for *main idea,* B for *too broad,* and N for *too narrow.*

_____ a. The UN created OCHA to deal with the human problems caused by conflict and natural disaster.

_____ b. OCHA collects donations and provides aid to victims of natural disasters.

_____ c. The United Nations is concerned with health, education, and economic development, as well as world peace.

Correct Answers, Part A _____

Correct Answers, Part B _____

Total Correct Answers _____

The Confederated Tribes of the Umatilla Indian Reservation

The area encompassing southeastern Washington, northeastern Oregon, and western Idaho is known as the Columbia Plateau. The Plateau covers more than 6.4 million acres of rivers, forested mountains, and lush valleys. Before 1855, it was home to various Native American groups. The Cayuse, Umatilla, and Walla Walla people spoke different but related languages, and they followed similar ways of life but had different customs and traditions. They traveled with the seasons of the year. They fished for salmon in the spring, hunted deer and elk and harvested roots and berries in the summer, and sought the mild climate of the valleys in the winter.

In the mid-1840s, with the opening of the Oregon Trail, the number of settlers who had been seeking opportunity along the Pacific coast increased dramatically. To promote settlement and bring these territories into the Union, the United States government reserved for Native American groups some smaller areas as permanent homelands. Native Americans could avoid conflicts with incoming settlers by moving.

Through the Treaty of 1855, the Cayuse, Umatilla, and Walla Walla people accepted a property, the Umatilla Indian Reservation, in northeast Oregon. They also reserved the right to fish, hunt, and gather traditional foods both on and off their land. Later laws that were passed by the U.S. government reduced the size of the reservation. Today the Umatilla Indian Reservation includes about 172,000 acres of land.

The idea of a reservation was not the only thing new to these Native Americans. Also unfamiliar was the concept of the *confederation of tribes.* The bands that made up the Cayuse, Umatilla, and Walla Walla nations had camped together during the winter but had gone their separate ways during the food-gathering season. These small bands, each with its own leader, did not regard themselves as members of a larger nation. Tribal names, which grouped certain bands together, were an invention of nonnative explorers and settlers who identified family groups or bands living near one another with a place name. Thus, the unique bands living in the Umatilla area became known as the Umatilla Nation.

The Confederated Tribes of the Umatilla Reservation wrote and adopted a constitution and a set of by-laws that was approved by the U.S. Secretary of the Interior in 1949. After years of intermarriage and social and economic integration, distinctions between the three main groups of the confederation have decreased.

Reading Time _____

Recalling Facts

1. Through the Treaty of 1855, the Cayuse, Umatilla, and Walla Walla
   - ❏ a. ended a thirty-year border dispute between them.
   - ❏ b. moved to the Umatilla Indian Reservation.
   - ❏ c. agreed to hunt and fish only in an officially designated area.

2. The traditional way of life for the Cayuse, Umatilla, and Walla Walla people included
   - ❏ a. fishing, farming, and hunting.
   - ❏ b. fishing for trout and hunting elk.
   - ❏ c. fishing, hunting, and harvesting wild plants.

3. The U.S. government moved to put the Cayuse, Umatilla, and Walla Walla people on a reservation
   - ❏ a. after the opening of the Oregon Trail.
   - ❏ b. after the Treaty of 1855.
   - ❏ c. as part of the Indian Reorganization Act of 1934.

4. The identification of these Native American groups as tribes
   - ❏ a. came from non-Indian explorers and settlers.
   - ❏ b. evolved as part of their cultural traditions.
   - ❏ c. originated with the leaders of the smaller groups or bands.

5. The government of the Confederated Tribes today
   - ❏ a. was established by the U.S. government.
   - ❏ b. replicates systems in use before 1855.
   - ❏ c. is based on a constitution and by-laws approved in 1949.

Understanding Ideas

6. One can conclude that the Confederated Tribes
   - ❏ a. benefited greatly from the Treaty of 1855.
   - ❏ b. gave up much of their freedom in the Treaty of 1855.
   - ❏ c. looked forward to satisfying the Treaty of 1855.

7. One might conclude from this passage that the opening of the Oregon Trail
   - ❏ a. caused profound changes for Native Americans in the area.
   - ❏ b. provided new opportunities for Native American groups.
   - ❏ c. caused minor changes in the natives' social patterns.

8. It seems likely, according to this passage, that most settlers
   - ❏ a. looked forward to having contact with Native Americans.
   - ❏ b. saw few, if any, differences between the various groups of Native Americans.
   - ❏ c. realized early on that in each group of Native Americans a distinctive culture had evolved.

9. This passage suggests that the region of the Columbia Plateau was rich in
   - ❏ a. minerals and fish.
   - ❏ b. timber and minerals.
   - ❏ c. fish and timber.

10. With the treaty of 1855, one of the greatest changes the Confederated Tribes would have to adapt to may have been a society that
    - ❏ a. migrated only twice a year.
    - ❏ b. had to live in only one place.
    - ❏ c. was located far from its traditional homeland.

5	B	The Search for Prosperity: Business on the Reservation

The impulse to honor one's culture is a fundamental one that has many benefits. It can even result in an improved economy, which was indeed the case for the Confederated Tribes of the Umatilla Indian Reservation (CTUIR).

In the 1980s, the CTUIR faced serious financial problems. Tribal leaders and members looked for ways to alleviate them and turned to tourism as one solution, planning a complex that would include a museum, a motel, a restaurant, a recreational vehicle park, a golf course, and a gaming center.

The approach was excellent. Between 1992 and 2002, with the construction of the Wildhorse Resort and Casino, the unemployment rate plummeted from 37 percent to 17 percent. The number of people hired rose from 159 to 1,138, and the yearly payroll increased almost tenfold—from $2.5 million to $24 million. Income generated by the resort has been a significant factor in the growth of new commercial businesses.

A key element of the complex is the Tamastslikt Cultural Center, which opened after the resort and casino. Situated not far from the Umatilla River, the center tells the story of the dramatic impact of the Oregon Trail on the Native American groups that lived in the area. The center features permanent and changing exhibits in the museum, educational programs, a theater, and a boutique selling Native American arts.

1. **Recognizing Words in Context**

   Find the word *alleviate* in the passage. One definition below is closest to the meaning of that word. One definition has the opposite or nearly the opposite meaning. The remaining definition has a completely different meaning. Label the definitions C for *closest*, O for *opposite or nearly opposite*, and D for *different*.

   _____ a. reduce

   _____ b. dislike

   _____ c. increase

2. **Distinguishing Fact from Opinion**

   Two of the statements below present *facts*, which can be proved. The other statement is an *opinion*, which expresses someone's thoughts or beliefs. Label the statements F for *fact* and O for *opinion*.

   _____ a. The Wildhorse Resort increased employment on the reservation.

   _____ b. The CTUIR plan was the best solution to the reservation's problems.

   _____ c. The education programs at the Cultural Center help others understand Native American history.

3. Keeping Events in Order

Number the statements below 1, 2, and 3 to show the order in which the events took place.

_____ a. The Wildhorse Resort and Casino was planned.

_____ b. The Tamastslikt Cultural Center was built.

_____ c. The CTUIR faced serious economic problems.

4. Making Correct Inferences

Two of the statements below are correct *inferences,* or reasonable guesses. They are based on information in the passage. The other statement is an incorrect, or faulty, inference. Label the statements C for *correct* inference and F for *faulty* inference.

_____ a. The CTUIR is both an entertainment and an education facility for tourists.

_____ b. The strategy that the CTUIR used to solve the economic problem of unemployment was successful.

_____ c. The same strategy that the CTUIR used would be successful with any group, in any location.

5. Understanding Main Ideas

One of the statements below expresses the main idea of the passage. One statement is too general, or too broad. The other explains only part of the passage; it is too narrow. Label the statements M for *main idea,* B for *too broad,* and N for *too narrow.*

_____ a. Many Native American groups have been plagued for many years by serious economic problems.

_____ b. The CTUIR created a successful long-range plan for the economy of the reservation.

_____ c. The CTUIR included a cultural center in its resort complex.

Correct Answers, Part A _____

Correct Answers, Part B _____

Total Correct Answers _____

Who Writes the President's Speeches?

The president of the United States must be an orator. The president gives an annual address on the State of the Union and speaks at the inauguration and other special events. Presidential speeches are a part of American history. In his Gettysburg Address, Abraham Lincoln spoke fewer than 300 words, but those words have become immortal. Franklin D. Roosevelt set the standard for later presidents in his 30 "fireside chats," which aired on the radio and dealt with the Great Depression and World War II.

Beginning with George Washington, American presidents often sought assistance with the content and wording of their speeches, although they may have done the writing themselves. As time went on, the particular expertise of professional writers became more and more important. The first president to assign the task of speechwriting to an aide, however, was Calvin Coolidge (1923–1929), the laconic president whose nickname was "Silent Cal." The aide's name was Judson Welliver. (Today, there is a bipartisan organization for former presidential speechwriters, the Judson Welliver Society.) Since the middle of the twentieth century, the role of such speechwriters has expanded; the Executive branch now includes an Office of Speechwriting as part of its Department of Communications, Speechwriting, and Media Affairs.

It is the writers, moreover, who often craft the memorable words by which the public identifies a modern president. In his inaugural speech, John F. Kennedy urged Americans, "Ask not what your country can do for you—ask what you can do for your country." George H. W. Bush, in his inaugural speech, imagined community volunteers and organizations as "a thousand points of light." Both of these phrases originated with the gifted men and women who worked as the president's speechwriters.

The process of drafting a presidential speech is long and complicated, and different presidents make different contributions. Some write large portions of the text and invite criticism from aides and advisors; others ask speechwriters to draft a speech in its entirety, and then they edit it to their own satisfaction. In any case, speechwriting is a back-and-forth process involving specialists in the subject area addressed, the president's personal advisors, and (of course) the president. The final product, whatever the process, must "sound" like the person who speaks the words. As one speechwriter recently said, "Our concern was not to write a good speech, but to write a good speech that is also his speech."

Reading Time _____

Recalling Facts

1. When preparing a speech, most presidents
   - ❑ a. turn the entire matter over to the speechwriters.
   - ❑ b. do all of the writing themselves.
   - ❑ c. depend on advice from others about the wording and content.

2. The role of speechwriters in presidential speeches
   - ❑ a. had declined at the end of the twentieth century.
   - ❑ b. has expanded since the middle of the twentieth century.
   - ❑ c. is about the same for recent presidents as it was for George Washington.

3. The Office of Speechwriting
   - ❑ a. is part of the Executive branch of the U.S. government.
   - ❑ b. originated with the Calvin Coolidge administration.
   - ❑ c. began with the presidency of George Washington.

4. The phrase describing volunteers as "a thousand points of light" was written for the inaugural speech of
   - ❑ a. George H. W. Bush.
   - ❑ b. John F. Kennedy.
   - ❑ c. Franklin D. Roosevelt.

5. Judson Welliver was
   - ❑ a. responsible for writing Franklin D. Roosevelt's "fireside chats."
   - ❑ b. the first official presidential speechwriter.
   - ❑ c. the person who gave Calvin Coolidge the nickname of "Silent Cal."

Understanding Ideas

6. One can infer that speeches are an important means by which
   - ❑ a. a president communicates directly to the people.
   - ❑ b. people can learn about current events.
   - ❑ c. a president can control the media.

7. One can determine through context that a laconic person
   - ❑ a. might be called talkative.
   - ❑ b. probably has a quick wit.
   - ❑ c. is a person of few words.

8. One might infer from this passage that presidential speechwriters
   - ❑ a. should have a gift for wording memorable phrases.
   - ❑ b. do not need to be familiar with the president for whom the speech will be written.
   - ❑ c. are likely to expect wide public recognition for their endeavors.

9. Which of the following considerations would probably be least important to a presidential speechwriter?
   - ❑ a. Language patterns that are similar to the president's own way of talking.
   - ❑ b. Unusual words that demonstrate how intelligent the president is.
   - ❑ c. Arguments that prove the president's point of view.

10. One could conclude that
    - ❑ a. most presidents find it easy to communicate through words.
    - ❑ b. not all presidents are gifted speechwriters.
    - ❑ c. the most successful presidents have been the best speechwriters.

One Man Behind the Words: J. Terry Edmonds, Presidential Speechwriter

When people hear a president speak, they rarely think about others helping to shape the presentation. Today, however, presidents depend on writers such as J. Terry Edmonds to help them communicate effectively. Edmonds is the first African American ever to work as a full-time speechwriter for a U.S. president; he is also the first African American to serve as director of speechwriting for the White House. His is an all-American story of success.

Edmonds grew up in Baltimore, Maryland; his father drove a truck, and his mother worked as a waitress. A voracious reader, Edmonds demonstrated a gift for writing at his high school, Baltimore City College. After graduating in 1967, Edmonds went on to Morgan State University.

Edmonds began his career in business, with jobs in public relations and communications. He joined the world of politics as press secretary for his congressman from Baltimore. During President Bill Clinton's administration, he wrote speeches for Health and Human Services Secretary Donna Shalala and worked in a number of jobs in the White House and in federal offices. President Clinton then appointed him to the office of director of speech-writing. Following the 2000 elections, Edmonds returned to Morgan State University as the school's special assistant to the president for 2001–2002.

1. Recognizing Words in Context

Find the word *voracious* in the passage. One definition below is closest to the meaning of that word. One definition has the opposite or nearly the opposite meaning. The remaining definition has a completely different meaning. Label the definitions C for *closest*, O for *opposite or nearly opposite*, and D for *different*.

_____ a. oppressive

_____ b. reluctant

_____ c. avid

2. Distinguishing Fact from Opinion

Two of the statements below present *facts*, which can be proved. The other statement is an *opinion*, which expresses someone's thoughts or beliefs. Label the statements F for *fact* and O for *opinion*.

_____ a. Edmonds's life as a speech-writer is an all-American story of success.

_____ b. A president hires speech-writers to communicate more effectively.

_____ c. Edmonds left his job at the White House at the end of the Clinton Administration.

3. Keeping Events in Order

Number the statements below 1, 2, and 3 to show the order in which the events took place.

_____ a. Edmonds becomes press secretary for a U.S. congressman.

_____ b. Edmonds serves as director of speechwriting in the White House.

_____ c. Edmonds takes jobs in several governmental departments.

4. Making Correct Inferences

Two of the statements below are correct *inferences,* or reasonable guesses. They are based on information in the passage. The other statement is an incorrect, or faulty, inference. Label the statements C for *correct* inference and F for *faulty* inference.

_____ a. Edmonds's career advanced as a result of his exceptional skills in written communication.

_____ b. Speechwriters are not able to work for more than one person who holds a political office.

_____ c. Excellent writing skills are as valuable in business as they are in government.

5. Understanding Main Ideas

One of the statements below expresses the main idea of the passage. One statement is too general, or too broad. The other explains only part of the passage; it is too narrow. Label the statements M for *main idea,* B for *too broad,* and N for *too narrow.*

_____ a. Speechwriters help shape presidential addresses to the nation.

_____ b. Edmonds came from an ordinary Baltimore family and became a speechwriter for a U.S. president.

_____ c. Edmonds showed a gift for writing while he was in high school.

Correct Answers, Part A _____

Correct Answers, Part B _____

Total Correct Answers _____

Three Writers of World War I

People called World War I "the war to end all wars." Hostilities began in Western Europe and included European colonies in Asia and Africa. Russia was involved, as were Australia, New Zealand, Canada, and the United States.

Writers from every literary field documented their war experiences. Many who died on the battlefields were immortalized in poetry and prose. Others survived to publish some of the most compelling descriptions of war ever penned. Among the latter were German novelist Erich Maria Remarque, English poet and critic Robert Graves, and American journalist Thomas M. Johnson.

Remarque's 1929 novel, *All Quiet on the Western Front,* is perhaps the best-known story of World War I. Drawing heavily on Remarque's own experience as a German soldier, this story of friendships, hardships, and the human cost of all wars was adapted as a film in 1930.

When Graves published his memoir *Good-bye to All That* in 1929, it drew criticism as unpatriotic. Graves was 19 years old when he enlisted in the British army at the outbreak of World War I. Commissioned as an officer, Graves led his men through unimaginable horror in the battlefields—gas attacks, foul conditions in the trenches, and inept leadership by superior officers. Graves almost died after being wounded by shrapnel. His book is notable for its cynical tone, its sympathetic attitude toward the enlisted men, and its mockery of the English military system.

A newspaper correspondent rather than a soldier, Johnson, coauthor of *The Lost Battalion* (1938), reported on the war for the *New York Sun. The Lost Battalion* describes the fate of a group of soldiers under the command of Major Charles W. Whittlesey. The unit belonged to the American Expeditionary Forces, as the U.S. troops were called, and had been assigned to take and hold a position deep in German-held territory in France. The soldiers succeeded in reaching the position, but they had lost contact with headquarters. Misinformed about the soldiers' precise location, American airplane pilots dropped food and ammunition over German positions instead. An American artillery unit then attacked "the lost battalion" where they had hunkered down; more than 80 men died from this "friendly fire." Fewer than 200 of the original 554 men in the battalion survived the five-day ordeal.

These three works, along with many others, illustrated aspects of World War I from different perspectives and helped to present a balanced view of the war experience.

Reading Time _____

Recalling Facts

1. World War I was called
   - ❏ a. "the great war."
   - ❏ b. "the war to end all wars."
   - ❏ c. "the war of the worlds."

2. Perhaps the best-known story about World War I is
   - ❏ a. *The Lost Battalion.*
   - ❏ b. *Good-bye to All That.*
   - ❏ c. *All Quiet on the Western Front.*

3. Robert Graves was known to many as a
   - ❏ a. poet.
   - ❏ b. journalist.
   - ❏ c. humorist.

4. *The Lost Battalion* was an account of
   - ❏ a. an English military division.
   - ❏ b. an American military unit.
   - ❏ c. a French military company.

5. Erich Maria Remarque was
   - ❏ a. a news correspondent and soldier.
   - ❏ b. an American poet and soldier.
   - ❏ c. a German novelist and soldier.

Understanding Ideas

6. One can infer that in World War I
   - ❏ a. the German army occupied French territory.
   - ❏ b. the American Expeditionary Forces fought against France.
   - ❏ c. communication across enemy lines was not problematic.

7. One might infer that
   - ❏ a. most of the literary works about World War I are memoirs.
   - ❏ b. journalists provided the most important written documents about the war.
   - ❏ c. writers used various genres to tell about their experiences of World War I.

8. All three literary works mentioned
   - ❏ a. were written by journalists.
   - ❏ b. describe the hardships and dangers of battle.
   - ❏ c. present flattering portraits of the military leadership.

9. One can infer that some people would have been critical of Graves's book because
   - ❏ a. it was sympathetic to the ordinary soldier.
   - ❏ b. it was published more than 10 years after the war ended.
   - ❏ c. it presented his country's military leaders in a bad light.

10. "Friendly fire" is
   - ❏ a. an attack by an enemy who pretends to be friendly.
   - ❏ b. a situation in which soldiers mistakenly attack people who are on their own side.
   - ❏ c. an attack against an enemy who used to be a friend.

What Did You Do in the War, Grandfather?

As a volunteer in the American Field Service, Jerome Preston experienced World War I at first hand from the driver's seat of an ambulance. In February 1917 Preston, 18 years old, departed for Paris.

Mastering the complicated shifting mechanisms of the Model-T Ford was Preston's first achievement; then he learned how to replace broken axles, change flat tires, and keep an engine running. Between battles he scrubbed the ambulance he named Kentucky, removing the mud and blood that his wounded passengers had left behind. Drivers earned the equivalent of five cents per day for exposing themselves to artillery fire and poisonous gas attacks. Each day they evacuated casualties all along the western front; in all, 127 of them died trying to save lives.

In 2002 Preston's granddaughter retraced his route in an effort to share his experience. She learned about places he had been from his diaries and identified them on a map. On her journey, she located the village near Verdun where Preston had lived in a farmhouse partially demolished by shells, she stopped at the bend in the road that the drivers called "Hell's Corner," and she located churches and restaurants that he had visited. She learned to appreciate the courage that twice earned her grandfather the French medal *Croix de Guerre*, or Cross of War.

1. **Recognizing Words in Context**

   Find the word *evacuated* in the passage. One definition below is closest to the meaning of that word. One definition has the opposite or nearly the opposite meaning. The remaining definition has a completely different meaning. Label the definitions C for *closest,* O for *opposite or nearly opposite,* and D for *different.*

   _____ a. retained

   _____ b ignored

   _____ c. removed

2. **Distinguishing Fact from Opinion**

   Two of the statements below present *facts,* which can be proved. The other statement is an *opinion,* which expresses someone's thoughts or beliefs. Label the statements F for *fact* and O for *opinion.*

   _____ a. Jerome Preston had to learn how to repair his ambulance and also had to keep it scrubbed clean.

   _____ b. Mastering the shifting mechanism of the Model-T was a great achievement.

   _____ c. Jerome Preston was working on the western front.

3. Keeping Events in Order

Number the statements below 1, 2, and 3 to show the order in which the events took place.

_____ a. Jerome Preston twice won the *Croix de Guerre.*

_____ b Jerome Preston volunteered as a member of the American Ambulance Field Service.

_____ c. Jerome Preston named his ambulance Kentucky.

4. Making Correct Inferences

Two of the statements below are correct *inferences,* or reasonable guesses. They are based on information in the passage. The other statement is an incorrect, or faulty, inference. Label the statements C for *correct* inference and F for *faulty* inference.

_____ a. Ambulances often broke down on the road.

_____ b. Jerome Preston sometimes lived in very uncomfortable circumstances.

_____ c. Jerome Preston spent much of his time in France learning about French culture.

5. Understanding Main Ideas

One of the statements below expresses the main idea of the passage. One statement is too general, or too broad. The other explains only part of the passage; it is too narrow. Label the statements M for *main idea,* B for *too broad,* and N for *too narrow.*

_____ a. Jerome Preston was awarded two *Croix de Guerres.*

_____ b. Thanks to Jerome Preston's written record of his life as a World War I ambulance driver, we know a great deal about his experiences.

_____ c. Many people volunteered to help the war effort.

Correct Answers, Part A _____

Correct Answers, Part B _____

Total Correct Answers _____

Tibet: The "Roof on the World"

Located in the midst of the nations of India, Nepal, Myanmar, Bhutan, and China, Tibet has a unique culture that reflects its history as a crossroads of the ancient world. Its remarkable geography includes a wide central plateau ringed by mountain ranges, which makes the country seem to float between earth and sky. Sometimes referred to as the "roof on the world," Tibet is the highest region on the planet. Southern Tibet lies within the Himalayas, which include peaks of dizzying height. The tallest of these is Mount Everest, which at 29,035 feet is also the tallest mountain in the world.

Tibet is a country that has been subject to positive foreign influences as well as military invasions. More than 1,400 years ago, the religious practice called Buddhism was introduced to Tibet from India, and at the same time the Sanskrit alphabet and other alphabets were adapted for use with the spoken Tibetan language. This was also the point in time when Tibet allied itself politically to both Nepal and China with the king's marriage to a princess from each of those countries. At the beginning of the thirteenth century, Mongol armies from the north swept through Asia, bringing both China and Tibet under their control.

For the next 600 years, Tibet remained closely associated with both China and Mongolia. At the beginning of the twentieth century, Tibet proclaimed its independence, but its sovereignty proved short-lived. In 1949 the People's Republic of China invaded Tibet. The country is now known officially as the Tibet Autonomous Region (TAR). The international debate on the legitimacy of the Chinese government in Tibet continues to the present.

In Tibetan culture, spirituality and Tibetan Buddhism (also known as Lamaism) exert great influence over daily life. The spiritual leader of Tibetan Buddhists is the Dalai Lama, a title that means "ocean of wisdom." The Dalai Lama's followers believe that he is the reincarnation of the Bodhisattva of Compassion, a deity regarded as the ancestor of the Tibetan people. The Potala Palace in Lhasa, Tibet, is a sacred location and the winter palace of the Dalai Lama. The palace itself is a symbol of the traditional role played by the Dalai Lama in the past in the Tibetan government. The present Dalai Lama, the fourteenth in the line of succession, has lived in exile in India since Tibet's revolt against Chinese rule in 1959. In 1989 he received the Nobel Peace Prize.

Reading Time _____

Recalling Facts

1. Tibet is bordered by the countries of
   - ❑ a. Mayanmar, Bhutan, Nepal, China, and India.
   - ❑ b. Mongolia, India, Bhutan, Nepal, and China.
   - ❑ c. India, Lhasa, Mongolia, Myanmar, and Nepal.

2. Tibet is called the "roof on the world" because it
   - ❑ a. provides most of the roofing materials used in the world.
   - ❑ b. is peaked in the center like a roof.
   - ❑ c. includes the highest region on Earth.

3. The religion of Buddhism was
   - ❑ a. introduced to Tibet from Mongolia less than 600 years ago.
   - ❑ b. introduced to Tibet from India more than 1,400 years ago.
   - ❑ c. eliminated by the army of the People's Republic of China.

4. The Dalai Lama
   - ❑ a. is the spiritual leader of Tibetan Buddhists.
   - ❑ b. is the elected representative of the TAR.
   - ❑ c. lives today in the Potala Palace in Lhasa, Tibet.

5. Tibet has often been
   - ❑ a. ignored by most of the countries in the region.
   - ❑ b. described as a country with no culture of its own.
   - ❑ c. subject to foreign influences and invasion.

Understanding Ideas

6. From reading this passage, one can conclude that
   - ❑ a. the high mountains of Tibet did not protect it from invading armies.
   - ❑ b. most Tibetans live in the city of Lhasa.
   - ❑ c. Tibet dominates most of the countries in the region.

7. According to this passage, a bodhisattva
   - ❑ a. is a kind of god.
   - ❑ b. is a descendent of the first Dalai Llama.
   - ❑ c. participates in the Tibetan government.

8. One might infer that Lamaism
   - ❑ a. is not practiced today in Tibet.
   - ❑ b. promotes peace among its followers.
   - ❑ c. is in direct conflict with Tibetan Buddhism.

9. According to the passage, which of these statements is the most valid?
   - ❑ a. Tibet shares a common culture with China.
   - ❑ b. China works with the Dalai Lama to govern Tibet.
   - ❑ c. Some people and nations do not accept China's right to make Tibet part of its territory.

10. One could infer from this passage that the Dalai Lama
    - ❑ a. maintains close ties with the People's Republic of China.
    - ❑ b. continues a leadership role, even in exile.
    - ❑ c. plays an insignificant role in nonreligious matters.

8   B   Ladakh

High in the Himalayas, at the eastern end of Kashmir, lies the dramatic landscape of Ladakh. Sometimes referred to as "Little Tibet" for its cultural and geographical affinities to the Tibet Autonomous Region of China, Ladakh was an independent kingdom for nearly 900 years. Since the middle of the twentieth century, however, governance has been shared among neighboring nations: India on the south, Pakistan on the north, and China on the east.

In ancient times, Ladakh offered the best and safest trade route from the Indian Punjab to Central Asia: countless caravans carrying spices and textiles crossed its terrain. The city of Leh became a busy crossroads, lively with bazaars and visitors from many countries. Ladakh was also the door through which first Buddhism and then Islam traveled eastward.

Deeply embedded in the culture of Ladakh are the sports of archery and polo. Summer archery festivals in Leh and the surrounding villages are highly competitive but are governed by strict rules of behavior. The contests are accompanied by the music of drums and the oboelike *surna;* dancing and other forms of entertainment are also part of the festivals. Polo is a more recent arrival and was probably introduced during the 1600s. Unlike polo as it is played in the West, this game is popular with the poor as well as the rich.

1. **Recognizing Words in Context**

   Find the word *affinities* in the passage. One definition below is closest to the meaning of that word. One definition has the opposite or nearly the opposite meaning. The remaining definition has a completely different meaning. Label the definitions C for *closest,* O for *opposite or nearly opposite,* and D for *different.*

   _____ a. similarities

   _____ b incompatibilities

   _____ c. complications

2. **Distinguishing Fact from Opinion**

   Two of the statements below present *facts,* which can be proved. The other statement is an *opinion,* which expresses someone's thoughts or beliefs. Label the statements F for *fact* and O for *opinion.*

   _____ a. Ladakh was once an important trade route to Central Asia.

   _____ b. Archery is a popular sport in Ladakh.

   _____ c. Ladakh's mountainous landscape is awe inspiring.

3. Keeping Events in Order

Number the statements below 1, 2, and 3 to show the order in which the events took place.

_____ a. Polo becomes a popular sport in Ladakh.

_____ b Rule of Ladakh is shared by India, Pakistan, and China.

_____ c. A bazaar grows up in Leh because of caravan routes through the region.

4. Making Correct Inferences

Two of the statements below are correct *inferences,* or reasonable guesses. They are based on information in the passage. The other statement is an incorrect, or faulty, inference. Label the statements C for *correct* inference and F for *faulty* inference.

_____ a. Ladakh is a larger country than Tibet.

_____ b. Ladakh is no longer the powerful nation it once was.

_____ c. In Ladakh, archery is a much more ancient sport than polo.

5. Understanding Main Ideas

One of the statements below expresses the main idea of the passage. One statement is too general, or too broad. The other explains only part of the passage; it is too narrow. Label the statements M for *main idea,* B for *too broad,* and N for *too narrow.*

_____ a. There are many small countries in southeast Asia.

_____ b. There is an archery festival each summer in Leh.

_____ c. Ladakh culture reflects the country's history as an important caravan route to Central Asia.

Correct Answers, Part A _____

Correct Answers, Part B _____

Total Correct Answers _____

Civil Rights Struggles of the 1950s and 1960s

The story of the American Civil Rights Movement is filled with heroes, villains, and martyrs. In the late 1940s, two acts signaled the beginning of a movement that would grow stronger in the two decades to follow: first, President Harry S Truman ended segregation in the military by executive order in 1948; second, on January 5, 1949, he guaranteed civil rights for all Americans in his State of the Union address.

Changing laws is the first step to changing behavior. Activists in the struggle for civil rights were quick to realize and act upon this. In the 1950s, successful lawsuits opened the door to equality for African Americans. In 1954 the U.S. Supreme Court ended school segregation when it decided unanimously, in the Kansas case *Brown vs. the Board of Education,* that "separate" could never be "equal." The court ruled that segregation was unconstitutional. In 1955 Rosa Parks was arrested in Montgomery, Alabama, for refusing to give up her seat on the bus to a white man. Within days a local minister, Martin Luther King Jr., helped to organize a bus boycott. Within the year, the Supreme Court ruled that bus segregation also violated the constitution. Then, in 1957, President Dwight D. Eisenhower ordered the National Guard to Little Rock, Arkansas, to ensure that nine students chosen to integrate Central High School could pass safely by angry demonstrators and attend classes.

The 1960s were marked by progress but marred by demonstrations that sometimes grew violent. African Americans, later joined by white peers, held "sit-ins" at lunch counters to draw attention to businesses that refused to serve black customers. Others held "kneel-ins" on the steps of churches that refused to allow them to worship there. The enrollment of James Meredith in 1962 at the University of Mississippi caused a riot. Two students died. Medgar Evers, a leader in the National Association for the Advancement of Colored People, was killed by white supremacist Byron De La Beckwith in 1963. Among other victims of the violence were three young volunteers in the voter-registration effort. Michael Schwerner and Andrew Goodman were white; James Chaney was black.

In the March on Washington in 1963, two hundred thousand civil-rights supporters walked peacefully to the Lincoln Memorial where they heard King's *I Have a Dream* speech. Two years later in Selma, Alabama, state troopers attacked peaceful marchers with tear gas and batons on a day that became known as "Bloody Sunday."

Reading Time _____

Recalling Facts

1. President Truman
   - ❏ a. ordered the National Guard to Little Rock, Arkansas, in 1957.
   - ❏ b. ended segregation in the U.S. military in 1948.
   - ❏ c. supported continued segregation in the U.S. military.

2. The key idea in the ruling for *Brown vs. the Board of Education* is that
   - ❏ a. "separate" cannot be "equal."
   - ❏ b. equality must be provided for groups separately.
   - ❏ c. equality in education cannot be guaranteed.

3. Martin Luther King Jr. organized a boycott to protest the
   - ❏ a. segregation of schools in Kansas.
   - ❏ b. refusal of some businesses to serve African American customers.
   - ❏ c. arrest of Rosa Parks for refusing to give her seat on the bus to a white man.

4. The first African American to attend the University of Mississippi was
   - ❏ a. James Meredith.
   - ❏ b. Byron De La Beckwith.
   - ❏ c. James Chaney.

5. The March on Washington
   - ❏ a. took place in the early days of the Civil Rights Movement.
   - ❏ b. is sometimes called "Bloody Sunday."
   - ❏ c. was the setting for King's *I Have a Dream* speech.

Understanding Ideas

6. One can infer that in the 1950s
   - ❏ a. the U.S. Supreme Court was not concerned with civil rights.
   - ❏ b. laws had to be overturned by the courts in order to guarantee all people their civil rights.
   - ❏ c. schools were segregated only in Southern states.

7. One can conclude that
   - ❏ a. few people showed their support for the Civil Rights Movement.
   - ❏ b. only a small minority resisted the changes of the Civil Rights Movement.
   - ❏ c. civil-rights activists often faced violent opposition.

8. One can infer that in the 1950s and 1960s, African American students who integrated all-white schools
   - ❏ a. sometimes risked their safety.
   - ❏ b. frequently resorted to violence to gain admission.
   - ❏ c. went on to become leaders in the Civil Rights Movement.

9. A "sit-in" was intended to
   - ❏ a. draw attention to the unequal treatment of Americans of different races.
   - ❏ b. start a fight with those who witnessed such an event.
   - ❏ c. avoid confrontation with the authorities.

10. Which of the following would most likely be described as a *martyr* of the Civil Rights Movement?
    - ❏ a. Rosa Parks
    - ❏ b. Medgar Evers
    - ❏ c. James Meredith

9   B   Changing the World Through Peaceful Means

In modern times, several prominent leaders have advocated nonviolence as the only effective route to lasting change. One of these was Mohandas Gandhi, in India. Another was Martin Luther King Jr., in the United States.

Gandhi (1869–1948) joined the campaign for an independent India after World War I. He challenged Great Britain's right to rule through an approach called *satyagraha,* which means "truth and firmness." *Satyagraha* includes the concept of "civil disobedience"—the belief that people should refuse to obey unjust laws. It also promotes the idea of "passive resistance," the peaceful but persevering demonstration of disagreement with laws or government. Passive resistance requires absolute peacefulness—the lack of self-defense—in the face of ongoing threats and attack.

King (1929–1968) studied Gandhi's teachings and in 1957 helped found the Southern Christian Leadership Conference. This group was committed to nonviolent resistance to unjust laws and focused on winning and protecting civil rights for African Americans. Two years later, King traveled to India to learn more about *satyagraha.* He used its principles as a basis for his writings "Six Principles of Nonviolence" and "Six Steps of Nonviolent Social Change."

In a terrible irony, both Gandhi and King died at the hands of assassins— victims of the hatred and violence they had identified as their enemy.

1. **Recognizing Words in Context**

   Find the word *advocated* in the passage. One definition below is closest to the meaning of that word. One definition has the opposite or nearly the opposite meaning. The remaining definition has a completely different meaning. Label the definitions C for *closest,* O for *opposite or nearly opposite,* and D for *different.*

   _____ a. submitted

   _____ b. supported

   _____ c. opposed

2. **Distinguishing Fact from Opinion**

   Two of the statements below present *facts,* which can be proved. The other statement is an *opinion,* which expresses someone's thoughts or beliefs. Label the statements F for *fact* and O for *opinion.*

   _____ a. Passive resistance is the best way to bring about social change.

   _____ b. King admired Gandhi's ideas and leadership.

   _____ c. The Southern Christian Leadership Conference used methods developed and espoused by Gandhi.

3. Keeping Events in Order

Number the statements below 1, 2, and 3 to show the order in which the events took place.

_____ a. King traveled to India to learn more about *satyagraha*.

_____ b. King helped found the Southern Christian Leadership Conference.

_____ c. Gandhi joined the campaign for an independent India.

4. Making Correct Inferences

Two of the statements below are correct *inferences*, or reasonable guesses. They are based on information in the passage. The other statement is an incorrect, or faulty, inference. Label the statements C for *correct* inference and F for *faulty* inference.

_____ a. A person who engages in civil disobedience is breaking a law.

_____ b. The deaths of Gandhi and King put an end to nonviolence as a means for social change.

_____ c. The practice of nonviolent methods of social change require great self-control, strong beliefs, and a commitment to certain principles.

5. Understanding Main Ideas

One of the statements below expresses the main idea of the passage. One statement is too general, or too broad. The other explains only part of the passage; it is too narrow. Label the statements M for *main idea*, B for *too broad*, and N for *too narrow*.

_____ a. Gandhi and King believed in nonviolence as a way to bring about lasting social and political change.

_____ b. Gandhi and King were two great leaders of the twentieth century.

_____ c. Gandhi and King were assassinated for their beliefs.

Correct Answers, Part A _____

Correct Answers, Part B _____

Total Correct Answers _____

Picturing the American West

In 1867 the United States faced the task of rebuilding after the ravages of the Civil War, so it looked westward for the raw materials needed to fuel industrial growth. Geological surveys and mapping expeditions were set forth to explore this unfamiliar territory. These groups, in turn, hired mapmakers, scientists, cooks, drivers, and doctors. They also hired painters and photographers as part of the teams. Painters needed few supplies, making it relatively easy for them to travel in the wilderness, but photographers were not so lucky; they had to transport a fully stocked darkroom on these expeditions.

Until the late 1870s, most photographers used the difficult wet-collodion process. The first step was to wash a clean sheet of glass with a sticky mixture of *collodion* and chemicals. (Collodion or "gun-cotton" was a recent medical discovery used to cover wounds because the viscous solution turned into a protective film when dry.) After it was washed, the plate went into another bath that stopped the picture from getting darker. Finally, the glass negative was rinsed clean with fresh water. Printing a photograph from the negative had to wait until the photographer went back to the studio. The size of the negative depended on the size of the camera. Mammoth-plate negatives could be as large as 20 by 24 inches.

Imagine the challenge of taking photographs in the 1860s and 1870s in the remote western wilderness! Photographers jolted over rocky mountains and through rushing rivers. They baked in the blazing desert heat, with cameras, sheets of glass, and vats of chemicals. Bad weather, equipment failures, and accidents were frequent problems. Success in creating a negative did not guarantee the production of a photograph; plates still had to be safely transported back to the studio before the image could be printed on paper. A photographer could lug 120 pounds of equipment many miles to capture a magnificent view or an unusual formation only to have the fragile plate destroyed in transit.

When photographers were successful, however, the results were exquisite and much admired. Photographs were put on exhibition, and people bought albums filled with pictures by Timothy O'Sullivan, Carleton Watkins, and William Henry Jackson, among others. Jackson's photographs of Yellowstone's natural wonders, along with the paintings of fellow expeditionary Thomas Moran, even helped persuade Congress to preserve thousands of acres of this land in 1872 as the nation's first national park.

Reading Time _____

Recalling Facts

1. Survey teams sent out to map the West
   - ❑ a. hired mainly cartographers who would make maps.
   - ❑ b. worked in pairs.
   - ❑ c. included scientists, artists, and laborers.

2. Collodion
   - ❑ a. was light sensitive.
   - ❑ b. was used by doctors to cover wounds.
   - ❑ c. was used to keep guns in working order.

3. The creation of a good collodion negative
   - ❑ a. required several steps.
   - ❑ b. was the easiest part of a photographer's job.
   - ❑ c. was impossible in the wilderness.

4. Photographers who worked in the wilderness made prints
   - ❑ a. in the darkroom right after the negative was made.
   - ❑ b. on glass plates in the photographer's tent.
   - ❑ c. after the negatives were transported back to the studio.

5. Problems that were encountered by photographers on survey and mapping expeditions included
   - ❑ a. lack of technical training.
   - ❑ b. bad weather, equipment failures, and accidents.
   - ❑ c. poor management of the team's resources.

Understanding Ideas

6. One can infer that outdoor wilderness photography in the 1870s
   - ❑ a. required perseverance.
   - ❑ b. was a popular pastime.
   - ❑ c. was not so popular as painting.

7. One can infer that a photographer working on a survey expedition
   - ❑ a. disliked living in the city.
   - ❑ b. needed physical strength.
   - ❑ c. had attended art school.

8. The importance of Jackson's photographs is evidenced by
   - ❑ a. their role in the creation of the first national park.
   - ❑ b. his financial success.
   - ❑ c. his friendship with Thomas Moran.

9. Which of the following sentences best expresses the main idea?
   - ❑ a. Congress authorized surveys and mapping expeditions that included photographers.
   - ❑ b. Photographers during the 1860s and 1870s overcame many obstacles to produce beautiful images of the West.
   - ❑ c. Timothy O'Sullivan, William Henry Jackson, and Carleton Watkins took photographs of the West.

10. The author probably believes that
   - ❑ a. the pictures these photographers made may also be works of art.
   - ❑ b. photography is more effective than painting in documenting unfamiliar terrain.
   - ❑ c. William Henry Jackson was the most gifted of the photographers of this era.

Norman Rockwell and the Four Freedoms

Norman Rockwell's art has been dismissed by some as mere illustration and lionized by others as the purest expression of the American character. Born in New York City in 1894, Rockwell studied at several New York art schools. His skills as a draftsman and his thorough familiarity with the art of the great masters helped him achieve early success as a freelance magazine illustrator.

On January 6, 1941, President Franklin D. Roosevelt described four basic human freedoms in his State of the Union address to Congress: freedom of speech and expression, freedom of worship, freedom from want, and freedom from fear. Inspired by these words, Rockwell created four paintings in 1943 that he called The Four Freedoms series.

The paintings express complex ideas through simple images. *Freedom of Speech,* for instance, illustrates a New England town meeting in which a citizen is presenting his opinion. *Freedom from Want* shows a family gathered around the holiday table as the mother sets down an immense roasted turkey.

The *Saturday Evening Post* magazine first reproduced the paintings. The originals were later exhibited throughout the United States, raising more than $130 million for the World War II effort through the sale of war bonds.

Norman Rockwell's art continues to be popular to this day. His autobiography, *My Adventures as an Illustrator,* was published in 1959.

1. **Recognizing Words in Context**

   Find the word *lionized* in the passage. One definition below is closest to the meaning of that word. One definition has the opposite or nearly the opposite meaning. The remaining definition has a completely different meaning. Label the definitions C for *closest,* O for *opposite or nearly opposite,* and D for *different.*

   _____ a. criticized

   _____ b. celebrated

   _____ c. pacified

2. **Distinguishing Fact from Opinion**

   Two of the statements below present *facts,* which can be proved. The other statement is an *opinion,* which expresses someone's thoughts or beliefs. Label the statements F for *fact* and O for *opinion.*

   _____ a. The four freedoms were beliefs articulated by Franklin D. Roosevelt.

   _____ b. Rockwell has provided the best expression of the American character.

   _____ c. Rockwell's series, The Four Freedoms, raised $130 million for the war effort.

3. Keeping Events in Order

Number the statements below 1, 2, and 3 to show the order in which the events took place.

_____ a. Rockwell's pictures raise more than $130 million for the war effort.

_____ b. The Four Freedoms series is published in the *Saturday Evening Post.*

_____ c. Rockwell publishes his autobiography.

4. Making Correct Inferences

Two of the statements below are correct *inferences,* or reasonable guesses. They are based on information in the passage. The other statement is an incorrect, or faulty, inference. Label the statements C for *correct* inference and F for *faulty* inference.

_____ a. Some people draw a distinction between art and illustration.

_____ b. Rockwell was one of the most respected and popular American artists in the 1940s.

_____ c. Rockwell's paintings were displayed only in magazines.

5. Understanding Main Ideas

One of the statements below expresses the main idea of the passage. One statement is too general, or too broad. The other explains only part of the passage; it is too narrow. Label the statements M for *main idea,* B for *too broad,* and N for *too narrow.*

_____ a. Rockwell's paintings representing the four freedoms were inspired by Roosevelt.

_____ b. Rockwell was a successful American illustrator.

_____ c. Artist Rockwell was able to express complicated ideas through simple images, as he did in the series The Four Freedoms.

Correct Answers, Part A _____

Correct Answers, Part B _____

Total Correct Answers _____

Changing Hemlines: The Stock Market and Fashion

Through the years, some economic analysts have hypothesized that the stock market takes its cue from fashion magazines: that it goes up or down along with hemlines; that when times are good and spending expands, fabric shrinks. A mathematician might express the idea as an inverse ratio and say that when more money buys less clothing, good times will surely follow.

Individuals can weigh the facts that follow and decide for themselves whether the "hemline theory" has any merit and whether it is true that widespread wealth is related to risqué fashion.

At the beginning of the twentieth century, the market suffered brief downturns following the assassination of President William McKinley in 1901 and the San Francisco earthquake in 1907. Hemlines hovered at the ankle, but an improved economy in the years just before World War I was accompanied by a more relaxed approach to fashion. More comfortable undergarments also replaced the stiff corsetry of the nineteenth century.

During the Roaring Twenties, flappers bobbed their hair and shortened their skirts, exposing a considerable length of leg encased in modern, sheer hosiery. The Dow Jones Industrial Index saw a rise of 350 percent. Then, on October 29, 1929, the market crashed, sending the United States into the Great Depression. Hemlines slipped below the calf.

As the business picture improved, feminine knees came back into view for the first time in years. Soon, the market responded with nationalistic fervor to the entrance of the United States into World War II after the bombing of Pearl Harbor. Hemlines stayed patriotically short throughout the war to help conserve fabric.

During the prosperous 1960s, shorts shrank into hotpants, and skirts went to mini and then to micromini length, heading higher and higher along with the stock market and the astronauts. There is a saying, however, that "what goes up must come down." The market turned decidedly bearish, declining along with hemlines as the country moved into the 1970s. Skirts again began to descend modestly.

Except for a few insignificant setbacks, the 1980s and 1990s represented the longest sustained bull market the country had ever seen, and the Dow Jones average rose from less than 1,000 points to a high that reached almost 12,000 points. Hemlines shot up; tops were cropped almost out of existence; "less" clothing turned into "more" fashion as computers and the Internet put millions of dollars into uncounted pockets.

Reading Time _____

Recalling Facts

1. According to the "hemline theory,"
   - ❑ a. fabric shrinks when it is laundered.
   - ❑ b. the rise and fall of the stock market and the raising and lowering of hemlines are related.
   - ❑ c. people buy more clothes in good economic times.

2. During the Roaring Twenties,
   - ❑ a. flappers wore their hair and dresses long.
   - ❑ b. the Dow Jones Index saw a rise of 350 percent.
   - ❑ c. the economy remained at its World War I level.

3. The crash of the stock market on October 29, 1929, marked
   - ❑ a. an upswing in employment in America.
   - ❑ b. the beginning of a period of risqué fashions.
   - ❑ c. the beginning of the Great Depression.

4. Which of the following fashions was typical of the 1960s?
   - ❑ a. The miniskirt
   - ❑ b. The maxiskirt
   - ❑ c. Bobbed hair

5. The stock market of the 1980s and 1990s is described as a
   - ❑ a. risky market.
   - ❑ b. bear market.
   - ❑ c. bull market.

Understanding Ideas

6. In a bear market, the stock market
   - ❑ a. makes steady gains.
   - ❑ b. changes significantly from day to day.
   - ❑ c. loses points over a period of time.

7. An event such as the assassination of a president is likely to result in
   - ❑ a. a bull market.
   - ❑ b. a fall in the stock market.
   - ❑ c. shorter hemlines.

8. In this passage, the saying "what goes up must come down" suggests that
   - ❑ a. good economic times are likely to be followed by poorer times.
   - ❑ b. short hemlines can only be sustained for about a year.
   - ❑ c. the laws of gravity prevail.

9. One can infer from this passage that
   - ❑ a. fashion designers control the economy.
   - ❑ b. market forces and consumer behavior are strongly related.
   - ❑ c. a bear market causes Americans to behave irrationally.

10. Which of the following best expresses the main idea of the passage?
    - ❑ a. Fashion is related to the larger society, including the economy.
    - ❑ b. In the Roaring Twenties, people bobbed their hair and shortened their hemlines.
    - ❑ c. In the twentieth century, there seemed to be a connection between the state of the stock market and the length of hemlines.

11   B   A More Natural Approach: Dress Reform in the Victorian Era

The Victorian Era was a time of high morals and modest behavior and dress. Although fashionable men and women both adhered to rules that governed their attire, menswear was relatively comfortable. By contrast, the fashionable woman could hardly move. Her figure was squeezed into an hourglass shape with whalebone corsets. Undergarments—which first included petticoats and later a crinoline or underskirt reinforced with wood or wire—could weigh up to 14 pounds. The trailing skirts and long, tight sleeves of a woman's outer dress impeded activity. Etiquette books offered instruction on how to manage this costume so as to walk, sit, and dance with modesty and decorum.

In the United States, Mrs. Amelia Bloomer (1818–1894) designed baggy pants cuffed at the ankle that could be worn under a knee-length skirt, a style now called "bloomers." Although few women adopted the look, Bloomer's ideas won the approval of many progressive thinkers in the United States and abroad.

In 1881 socially prominent British women formed the Rational Dress Society in London. They believed that no woman should have to wear more than seven pounds of undergarments and decried the use of corsets that "deformed the figure." They also advocated a "bifurcated garment" suitable for athletic exercise, gardening, housework, or the workplace. They admired Mrs. Bloomer's costume.

1. **Recognizing Words in Context**

   Find the word *decorum* in the passage. One definition below is closest to the meaning of that word. One definition has the opposite or nearly the opposite meaning. The remaining definition has a completely different meaning. Label the definitions C for *closest,* O for *opposite or nearly opposite,* and D for *different.*

   _____ a. fashionable dress

   _____ b. improper conduct

   _____ c. appropriate behavior

2. **Distinguishing Fact from Opinion**

   Two of the statements below present *facts,* which can be proved. The other statement is an *opinion,* which expresses someone's thoughts or beliefs. Label the statements F for *fact* and O for *opinion.*

   _____ a. Upper-class Victorian women wore enormous amounts of clothing.

   _____ b. The Rational Dress Society encouraged women to dress more simply.

   _____ c. Proper Victorian attire was more ladylike than the new bloomers.

3. Keeping Events in Order

Number the statements below 1, 2, and 3 to show the order in which the events took place.

_____ a. The Rational Dress Society is founded in London.

_____ b. Mrs. Bloomer designs a costume that combines baggy trousers with a short skirt.

_____ c. The movements of women are impeded by corsets and the weight of clothing they wear.

4. Making Correct Inferences

Two of the statements below are correct *inferences,* or reasonable guesses. They are based on information in the passage. The other statement is an incorrect, or faulty, inference. Label the statements C for *correct* inference and F for *faulty* inference.

_____ a. Women were more open to dress reform than men were.

_____ b. A "bifurcated garment" would resemble trousers to some extent.

_____ c. A crinoline was a cagelike structure that supported a woman's skirts.

5. Understanding Main Ideas

One of the statements below expresses the main idea of the passage. One statement is too general, or too broad. The other explains only part of the passage; it is too narrow. Label the statements M for *main idea,* B for *too broad,* and N for *too narrow.*

_____ a. Women's fashions have changed dramatically over the centuries.

_____ b. Toward the end of the nineteenth century, reformers sought to make clothing more comfortable and practical for women.

_____ c. Mrs. Amelia Bloomer was an early leader in the effort to reform women's fashions in the nineteenth century.

Correct Answers, Part A _____

Correct Answers, Part B _____

Total Correct Answers _____

Aztlan and the Cities of Gold: The Intersection of Legends

It is not uncommon to find legends from disparate cultures that nonetheless share certain ideas. Similarities between the mythologies of the Aztec and the Spaniards not only are curious but have significant historical consequences.

According to Aztec legend, the seven sons of the god Iztac Mixcoatl had emerged from the viscera of the earth through seven caves and settled on the island of Aztlan. There these sons founded seven cities in which were born the seven nations of Nahua. The word Aztlan comes from the Nahua language and means "the place of the heron." According to Aztec myth, Aztlan glistened white as the heron's plumage.

The Aztec people dominated Mexico for almost a century before they surrendered to Spanish invaders in 1521. Originally known as the Mexica, they were a Nahua-speaking nation that lived in the north and northwest parts of the country. Both aggressive and nomadic, the Mexica were guided by a prediction that they would create a magnificent civilization in the midst of marshes, in a place where an eagle—with a serpent in its talons—perched on a cactus that grew from a rock. They settled on the swampy shore of Lake Texcoco in the southern area now called the Valley of Mexico and brought the other Nahua nations under their dominion. The Aztec indeed became both rich and powerful, but the legend of Aztlan, their ancestral home, stayed with them.

The Spaniards had their own legend of paradise, of distant cities filled with spiritual and material riches. When Spain came under Islamic rule in the seventh century, a group of Christian bishops was rumored to have taken the Church's treasures and sought sanctuary far away. Like the tribes of Nahua, the bishops were seven in number, and like Aztlan the bishops' refuge was an island.

Over time the Spaniards' seven mythical cities became one with the seven ancestral caves of Aztlan, and in 1540 Francisco Coronado set out to discover what many believed were literally "Cities of Gold." His journey lasted three years, during which time he sent volunteers as far as the Gulf of California and the Grand Canyon of the Colorado River. Coronado himself eventually reached the Arkansas River on the edge of the Great Plains, but he never found any gold or any great cities and left behind only a number of devastated Indian villages and an oral legend that even today refuses to die.

Reading Time _____

Recalling Facts

1. The Aztecs were the dominant civilization in Mexico
   - ❑ a. in the century before the arrival of Spanish explorers.
   - ❑ b. from the time they left their ancestral land of Aztlan.
   - ❑ c. in the century following the arrival of Spanish explorers.

2. Aztlan was believed to be
   - ❑ a. a place full of herons and eagles.
   - ❑ b. an island that was home to the Nahua-speaking people.
   - ❑ c. an island in Lake Texcoco in the Valley of Mexico.

3. The Aztec people
   - ❑ a. were aggressive and nomadic.
   - ❑ b. migrated to Spain in 1521.
   - ❑ c. discovered the Cities of Gold.

4. The Spanish legend of the Cities of Gold began as a story about
   - ❑ a. treasures stolen by Islamic invaders of Spain.
   - ❑ b. great cities beyond the Colorado River.
   - ❑ c. an island to which seven bishops fled with treasure.

5. On his expedition to find the Cities of Gold, Coronado
   - ❑ a. searched throughout the Valley of Mexico.
   - ❑ b. traveled as far as the Arkansas River.
   - ❑ c. set sail to some islands.

Understanding Ideas

6. One can infer from this passage that
   - ❑ a. Coronado wanted to recover treasures for the Church.
   - ❑ b. the Aztec people abandoned their belief in Aztlan.
   - ❑ c. legends can be an important part of a people's culture.

7. The best word to describe the similarities between the Aztec and Spanish legends in this passage is
   - ❑ a. coincidence.
   - ❑ b. destiny.
   - ❑ c. unique.

8. In contrast with the Spanish legend of the Cities of Gold, the Aztec belief in Aztlan was
   - ❑ a. not so influential.
   - ❑ b. more important before the Mexica settled in the Valley of Mexico.
   - ❑ c. a creation myth.

9. One can infer from this passage that
   - ❑ a. Native Americans prevented Coronado from finding the Cities of Gold.
   - ❑ b. some people still hope to find traces of the Cities of Gold.
   - ❑ c. the real Cities of Gold are on an island near Spain.

10. Which of the following statements best expresses the main idea?
    - ❑ a. The Aztec people dominated Mexico for almost a century.
    - ❑ b. Spaniards had their own legend: cities filled with riches.
    - ❑ c. Similar legends of the Aztec and Spaniards became one in the New World, prompting the explorations of Coronado.

Collecting Oral History

At first encounter in elementary and secondary school, history seems primarily about ancient events and achievements, the collision of powers, and the privileges of wealth. History, however, is personal as well as public: it is composed of intimate expressions as well as grand narratives, the lives of ordinary people as well as the doings of the famous.

Collecting oral history—conducting interviews—is one way to flesh out the bare bones of the larger record so as to develop a better and more thorough understanding of the past. Anyone can collect oral history. Guidance in conducting interviews is available from local historical societies or colleges or may be found at the library or on the Internet.

All of the foregoing resources recommend that researchers be prepared. Interviewers should develop a list of questions and send a copy of the list to the subject of the interview well in advance. A good questionnaire will begin with the basics of biography. Simple questions will allow the person being interviewed to focus on one idea at a time; the interviewer can pose a follow-up question, if needed. Finally, the interviewer should phrase the questions so that they cannot be answered by a simple yes or no and should also encourage digressions; sometimes a wide-ranging ramble can be more interesting and yield more information than a direct answer.

1. **Recognizing Words in Context**

Find the word combination *flesh out* in the passage. One definition below is closest to the meaning of that word. One definition has the opposite or nearly the opposite meaning. The remaining definition has a completely different meaning. Label the definitions C for *closest*, O for *opposite or nearly opposite*, and D for *different*.

_____ a. make fuller

_____ b. leave incomplete

_____ c. make over

2. **Distinguishing Fact from Opinion**

Two of the statements below present *facts*, which can be proved. The other statement is an *opinion*, which expresses someone's thoughts or beliefs. Label the statements F for *fact* and O for *opinion*.

_____ a. The basics of biography are the facts of a person's life.

_____ b. The interview should begin with biographical questions.

_____ c. Ancient events and cultural achievements are the usual focus of history books.

3. Keeping Events in Order

Number the statements below 1, 2, and 3 to show the order in which the events took place.

_____ a. The reviewer prepares a questionnaire.

_____ b. The reviewer encourages the subject to digress.

_____ c. The reviewer sends a copy of a questionnaire to the interviewee.

4. Making Correct Inferences

Two of the statements below are correct *inferences,* or reasonable guesses. They are based on information in the passage. The other statement is an incorrect, or faulty, inference. Label the statements C for *correct* inference and F for *faulty* inference.

_____ a. A person who collects oral history has a better understanding of the past than people who study history through other means.

_____ b. Oral history helps place large events, such as war, in the context of personal experience.

_____ c. Although there are ways to prepare to conduct an interview, no special training is required.

5. Understanding Main Ideas

One of the statements below expresses the main idea of the passage. One statement is too general, or too broad. The other explains only part of the passage; it is too narrow. Label the statements M for *main idea,* B for *too broad,* and N for *too narrow.*

_____ a. Following specific interviewing techniques can help a person use oral histories to develop a more thorough understanding of the past.

_____ b. Always prepare a list of questions before interviewing the subject of an oral history.

_____ c. History is both personal and public, and it can be about ordinary people as well as famous people.

Correct Answers, Part A _____

Correct Answers, Part B _____

Total Correct Answers _____

60

The first shots of the American Revolution were fired in Massachusetts in April 1775. Even before those shots rang out, women were part of the push for independence; scholars provide much evidence of women's involvement in political and economic acts as well as in combat and espionage.

Some colonial women were vocal in their opposition to British rule. Mercy Otis Warren, for instance, published seditious works that presented British rule as greedy, corrupt, and brutal. Other women organized boycotts of British goods, devising homemade substitutes for such imports as linen cloth, tea, and coffee. During the war, not only did women perform "traditional" female tasks such as nursing the wounded and sewing uniforms; they also took over traditionally male occupations, becoming weavers, carpenters, and blacksmiths. Patriotic societies such as the Daughters of Liberty raised money and made clothing for the Continental Army.

The daring and physical courage of many women put them in harm's way. Paul Revere was not the only one to ride through the countryside warning citizens of the approach of British troops. Sixteen-year-old Sybil Ludington was just as heroic. In 1777 she rode 40 miles in the black of night to rouse the militia following the British assault on a supply depot in Danbury, Connecticut. Women gathered intelligence on British movements and found ways to get this information to their local militias. Lydia Barrington Darragh, a mother of nine, sneaked through enemy lines to warn General George Washington of an ambush that had been planned. Teenager Susanna Bolling crossed the Appomattox River alone and at night to alert General Joseph Lafayette about an attack.

Some women even fought alongside the men. Among the most famous of these was Deborah Samson, who joined the fourth Massachusetts Regiment disguised as Robert Shirtliffe. She was wounded twice during three years of fighting, and her sex remained secret until she became ill with a brain fever. When Fort Washington, New York, was attacked in 1776, Margaret Cochran Corbin assisted her husband, John, in taking over a cannon from a gunner who had been killed. When John was killed, Margaret became the gunner until she was badly wounded. Eventually Congress awarded her a soldier's pension for her remarkable courage. Nancy Morgan Hart defended her Georgia cabin from a small group of soldiers sympathetic to the British side. She shot and killed one of the soldiers, and her later exploits as a spy became legendary.

Reading Time _____

Recalling Facts

1. The first shots of the American Revolution were fired in
   - ❏ a. New York.
   - ❏ b. Virginia.
   - ❏ c. Massachusetts.

2. Mercy Otis Warren
   - ❏ a. expressed her opposition to British rule through her writing.
   - ❏ b. was among the first women to fight in battle in the American Revolution.
   - ❏ c. believed in the justness of British rule in America.

3. The Daughters of Liberty
   - ❏ a. organized an espionage ring to assist the Continental Army.
   - ❏ b. published anti-British books and pamphlets.
   - ❏ c. sewed clothing and raised money for the Continental Army.

4. Deborah Samson
   - ❏ a. was famous during the American Revolution for providing food for soldiers.
   - ❏ b. fought in battle as a man under the identity of Robert Shirtliffe.
   - ❏ c. informed General Washington of a planned ambush.

5. An example of a "traditional" female activity during the American Revolution would be
   - ❏ a. conducting espionage.
   - ❏ b. nursing the wounded at the front lines.
   - ❏ c. working as a carpenter.

Understanding Ideas

6. One could infer from this passage that women were
   - ❏ a. not allowed to join the Continental Army.
   - ❏ b. discouraged from joining the Continental Army.
   - ❏ c. drafted into the Continental Army.

7. Most Americans would have regarded the purchase of boycotted goods such as tea as
   - ❏ a. necessary.
   - ❏ b. admirable.
   - ❏ c. unpatriotic.

8. One might conclude from this passage that
   - ❏ a. most Revolutionary War–era women were unfamiliar with guns and unable to protect themselves.
   - ❏ b. women could provide few kinds of assistance during the Revolutionary War.
   - ❏ c. many Revolutionary War–era women knew how to handle guns to protect themselves.

9. The women most opposed to British rule were
   - ❏ a. from no particular age group or social class.
   - ❏ b. teenage girls without families to care for.
   - ❏ c. educated women whose children were old enough to fight.

10. A piece of "seditious" writing would
    - ❏ a. poke fun at the behavior of the upper classes.
    - ❏ b. be critical of the government.
    - ❏ c. be unbiased in its opinions.

13   B   Anne Hutchinson: The Courage of Her Convictions

Anne Hutchinson was born in England in 1591. A woman of sincere spiritual convictions, who taught that each person's relationship with the divine was personal and private, she believed that salvation was received through grace and not through learning or adhering to dogma. Hutchinson left England for America in search of religious freedom, but her free-thinking ideas brought her into conflict with clergy members who wielded both religious and secular power in the Massachusetts Bay Colony.

The clergy attacked Hutchinson by punishing her followers. Then John Winthrop was elected governor, unseating a man who had been sympathetic to Hutchinson's ideas. Finally, Hutchinson herself was tried in court and found guilty of willfully misrepresenting Puritan teachings. The court banished her from the colony, and her family moved to what is now the state of Rhode Island. After the death of her husband, she settled in New York. In 1643 Hutchinson and all but one member of her family were attacked and killed by Native Americans.

Hutchinson was neither the first nor the last to face religious persecution in the nation's history. Despite threats of whippings, banishment, and even execution, commitment to religious freedom grew. In 1789 the U.S. Constitution established the first protection of religious rights, and the First Amendment expanded these protections when the Bill of Rights was ratified.

1. **Recognizing Words in Context**

   Find the word *wielded* in the passage. One definition below is closest to the meaning of that word. One definition has the opposite or nearly the opposite meaning. The remaining definition has a completely different meaning. Label the definitions C for *closest*, O for *opposite or nearly opposite*, and D for *different*.

   _____ a. accommodated to

   _____ b. omitted

   _____ c. exerted

2. **Distinguishing Fact from Opinion**

   Two of the statements below present *facts*, which can be proved. The other statement is an *opinion*, which expresses someone's thoughts or beliefs. Label the statements F for *fact* and O for *opinion*.

   _____ a. Hutchinson came to America in search of religious freedom.

   _____ b. Hutchinson was the most deeply spiritual woman of her time.

   _____ c. Hutchinson was found guilty of misrepresenting Puritan teachings.

3. Keeping Events in Order

Number the statements below 1, 2, and 3 to show the order in which the events took place.

_____ a. The U.S. Constitution, guaranteeing religious freedom, was written.

_____ b. The followers of Anne Hutchinson were punished.

_____ c. Anne Hutchinson settled in an area that is now called Rhode Island.

4. Making Correct Inferences

Two of the statements below are correct *inferences,* or reasonable guesses. They are based on information in the passage. The other statement is an incorrect, or faulty, inference. Label the statements C for *correct* inference and F for *faulty* inference.

_____ a. Religious freedom was unprotected until the Constitution established protection.

_____ b. The election of John Winthrop as governor was not a fair election.

_____ c. The clergy could be a powerful political force in colonial America.

5. Understanding Main Ideas

One of the statements below expresses the main idea of the passage. One statement is too general, or too broad. The other explains only part of the passage; it is too narrow. Label the statements M for *main idea,* B for *too broad,* and N for *too narrow.*

_____ a. Anne Hutchinson was put on trial in the colony for her beliefs.

_____ b. Anne Hutchinson's story is an important chapter in the history of religious freedom in America.

_____ c. Freedom of religion has not always been guaranteed in America.

Correct Answers, Part A _____

Correct Answers, Part B _____

Total Correct Answers _____

Interstate Highway System

To many car-crazy Americans, the world seems to be one long superhighway. A couple of generations ago, however, it was a different story.

In 1900 about 8,000 automobiles traveled on American roads. The roads themselves were little more than tracks scratched into the dirt. In fact, many "highways" were merely traces of old pioneer routes, such as the Oregon Trail. Paved roads were few in number and mostly found in cities; their surfaces were usually cobblestone. Road maintenance was all but nonexistent, and seasonal rains, winter's cold, and summer's dust could make roads impassable. As cars became more affordable, however, car ownership increased dramatically, and by 1916 nearly 2.5 million vehicles were in use. Both state and federal legislatures were pressured to create a system of roads, and ribbons of asphalt and concrete began to stretch across the countryside.

The U.S. Army was the first organization to investigate the idea of a national highway system. In 1919 the first Transcontinental Motor Convoy left Washington, D.C., headed for San Francisco. Its goal was to test the durability of a number of motor vehicles developed during World War I and to assess the challenges involved in moving an army over such a distance. A young lieutenant colonel named Dwight D. Eisenhower volunteered to join the convoy; it covered 3,251 miles in 62 days and moved at an average speed of 5 miles per hour. Young Ike (that was how Eisenhower was known to his friends) found the trip a genuine adventure and started to think about the importance of good paved highways to a nation's future. During the 1920s and 1930s, the country continued to move toward the creation of an interstate highway system similar to those already in place in other nations. As commander of the U.S. forces occupying Germany following World War II, Eisenhower, now a general, studied the *autobahns*—the excellent roads that crisscrossed that land.

President Eisenhower signed into law the Federal Aid Highway Act in 1956. While he was in office, the building of more than 45,000 miles of highways became the largest peacetime construction project ever carried out in the United States. In 1990 President George H. W. Bush signed legislation that renamed the highway system the Dwight D. Eisenhower System of Interstate and Defense Highways. Today, approximately 160,000 miles of roadways are included in the Eisenhower System and related arteries that together make up the National Highway System.

Reading Time _____

Recalling Facts

1. Many of the first "highways" were
   - ❏ a. built by the federal government.
   - ❏ b. traces of pioneer routes, such as the Oregon Trail.
   - ❏ c. paved with cobblestones.

2. When cars became more common,
   - ❏ a. state and federal governments were pressured into building more roads.
   - ❏ b. it was no longer necessary to argue about the importance of good roads.
   - ❏ c. people began to build private roads.

3. The first Transcontinental Motor Convoy
   - ❏ a. traveled to the West Coast on the Oregon Trail.
   - ❏ b. was under the command of Dwight D. Eisenhower.
   - ❏ c. was a group sent by the Army to drive from coast to coast.

4. President Eisenhower signed into law the _____ Act in 1956.
   - ❏ a. National Highway System
   - ❏ b. first Transcontinental Motor Convoy
   - ❏ c. Federal Aid Highway

5. Today there are approximately 160,000 miles of highways in the
   - ❏ a. Eisenhower System.
   - ❏ b. National Highway System.
   - ❏ c. United States and Canada.

Understanding Ideas

6. From reading the passage, one might conclude that
   - ❏ a. cars are a very important part of American culture.
   - ❏ b. the United States was a leader in building highway systems.
   - ❏ c. only the last few generations of Americans have cared about their cars.

7. One can conclude from this passage that Dwight D. Eisenhower
   - ❏ a. was not influenced by the achievements of other nations.
   - ❏ b. had a significant impact in developing a national highway system.
   - ❏ c. campaigned for an interstate highway system in 1919.

8. It seems likely that roads were not dependable throughout the year until
   - ❏ a. the federal government took them over.
   - ❏ b. after World War II.
   - ❏ c. they had been paved.

9. One can infer that Germany's roads during World War II were
   - ❏ a. the best in the world.
   - ❏ b. superior to U.S. roads.
   - ❏ c. as advanced as U.S. roads.

10. Which of the following sentences best expresses the main idea?
   - ❏ a. The Interstate Highway System turned poorly maintained roads into a network of well-kept highways.
   - ❏ b. Eisenhower studied the system of German autobahns.
   - ❏ c. The United States today seems to be one long superhighway.

Boston's MBTA and the Progress of Public Transportation

The Massachusetts Bay Transit Authority runs the oldest system of public transportation in the United States. It had its beginnings in 1631, when the government of the Massachusetts Bay Colony allowed Thomas Williams to run a ferry between Chelsea and Boston. This service changed a two-day ride over land into a three-mile trip across Boston Harbor. Travelers relied on ferries for another hundred years until bridges were built across the harbor and the Charles River.

It became a great deal easier to get from place to place in Boston during the 1800s. The omnibus was the first improvement. This horse-drawn wagon was lined with benches, and passengers could get on or off at various points along a set route. Later on, trolleys on railway tracks carried people throughout the city and into nearby towns. On New Year's Day in 1889, the first electric trolley was put into service. The first subway, or underground train, opened in Boston in 1897.

Since 1964 the Federal Transit Administration of the U.S. Department of Transportation has helped the MBTA grow. Economic problems, rising fuel costs, population growth, and concerns about air pollution in the 1970s have tested the MBTA's capacities. However, today the MBTA has trains, buses, and boats that serve 175 cities and cover more than 3,000 square miles in eastern Massachusetts.

1. **Recognizing Words in Context**

   Find the word *capacities* in the passage. One definition below is closest to the meaning of that word. One definition has the opposite or nearly the opposite meaning. The remaining definition has a completely different meaning. Label the definitions C for *closest*, O for *opposite or nearly opposite*, and D for *different*.

   _____ a. preferences

   _____ b. resources

   _____ c. inabilities

2. **Distinguishing Fact from Opinion**

   Two of the statements below present *facts*, which can be proved. The other statement is an *opinion*, which expresses someone's thoughts or beliefs. Label the statements F for *fact* and O for *opinion*.

   _____ a. The mass transportation system in Boston is the best in the United States.

   _____ b. The area served by the MBTA extends beyond the city limits of Boston.

   _____ c. The harbor once isolated Boston from other nearby towns.

3. Keeping Events in Order

Number the statements below 1, 2, and 3 to show the order in which the events took place.

_____ a. Underground trains go into service.

_____ b. A ferry service makes the trip from Chelsea to Boston faster.

_____ c. A horse-drawn vehicle called an omnibus carries people throughout Boston.

4. Making Correct Inferences

Two of the statements below are correct *inferences,* or reasonable guesses. They are based on information in the passage. The other statement is an incorrect, or faulty, inference. Label the statements C for *correct* inference and F for *faulty* inference.

_____ a. Transporting goods and people into Boston was difficult during the 1600s and 1700s.

_____ b. Mass transportation in Boston is more appreciated today than in earlier times.

_____ c. The U.S. government aids public transportation programs through the Federal Transit Administration.

5. Understanding Main Ideas

One of the statements below expresses the main idea of the passage. One statement is too general, or too broad. The other explains only part of the passage; it is too narrow. Label the statements M for *main idea,* B for *too broad,* and N for *too narrow.*

_____ a. Mass transit, important in Boston from its outset, has expanded and improved over the years.

_____ b. Mass transportation has been an important part of the development of cities in the United States.

_____ c. The ferry from Boston to Chelsea across the Charles River was an efficient means of transportation in the 1800s.

Correct Answers, Part A _____

Correct Answers, Part B _____

Total Correct Answers _____

15 A · Playing for Pay: Amateurs, Professionals, and the Olympic Games

The modern Olympic Games, founded in 1896, began as contests between individuals, rather than among nations, with the hope of promoting world peace through sportsmanship. In the beginning, the games were open only to amateurs. An *amateur* is a person whose involvement in an activity—from sports to science or the arts—is purely for pleasure. Amateurs, whatever their contributions to a field, expect to receive no form of compensation; professionals, in contrast, perform their work in order to earn a living.

From the perspective of many athletes, however, the Olympic playing field has been far from level. Restricting the Olympics to amateurs has precluded the participation of many who could not afford to be unpaid. Countries have always desired to send their best athletes, not their wealthiest ones, to the Olympic Games.

A slender and imprecise line separates what we call "financial support" from "earning money." Do athletes "earn money" if they are reimbursed for travel expenses? What if they are paid for time lost at work or if they accept free clothing from a manufacturer or if they teach sports for a living? The runner Eric Liddell was the son of poor missionaries; in 1924 the British Olympic Committee financed his trip to the Olympics, where he won a gold and a bronze medal. College scholarships and support from the United States Olympic Committee made it possible for American track stars Jesse Owens and Wilma Rudolph and speed skater Dan Jansen to train and compete. When the Soviet Union and its allies joined the games in 1952, the definition of *amateur* became still muddier. Their athletes did not have to balance jobs and training because as citizens in communist regimes, their government financial support was not considered payment for jobs.

In 1971 the International Olympic Committee (IOC) removed the word *amateur* from the rules, making it easier for athletes to find the support necessary to train and compete. In 1986 the IOC allowed professional athletes into the games.

There are those who regret the disappearance of amateurism from the Olympic Games. For them the games lost something special when they became just another way for athletes to earn money. Others say that the designation of amateurism was always questionable; they argue that all competitors receive so much financial support as to make them paid professionals. Most agree, however, that the debate over what constitutes an "amateur" will continue for a long time.

Reading Time _____

Recalling Facts

1. The Olympic Games were first intended to be
   - ❏ a. athletic contests between nations.
   - ❏ b. contests between the best athletes in the world.
   - ❏ c. contests between amateur athletes.

2. An amateur in a particular field
   - ❏ a. expects to become a professional one day.
   - ❏ b. does not expect to earn money at the sport that is played.
   - ❏ c. receives little respect from professionals in the same field.

3. Entrance of the Soviet Union into the Olympics resulted in
   - ❏ a. strife between the communist and noncommunist athletes.
   - ❏ b. more competitive games.
   - ❏ c. even less clarity about the definition of *amateur.*

4. Communist countries provided
   - ❏ a. support, so their athletes could train all year.
   - ❏ b. coaching jobs for athletes.
   - ❏ c. scholarships, so their athletes could go to college.

5. In 1971 the International Olympic Committee
   - ❏ a. eliminated professional athletes.
   - ❏ b. dropped the word *amateur* from the Olympic rules.
   - ❏ c. stopped allowing communists to participate.

Understanding Ideas

6. One might infer that
   - ❏ a. developing Olympic-level skills in athletes is costly.
   - ❏ b. professional athletes are mostly interested in financial rewards.
   - ❏ c. amateur athletes have a better attitude than professionals do.

7. The statement "the playing field has been far from level" means that
   - ❏ a. the ground the athletes played on was in bad condition.
   - ❏ b. the poorer players were given some advantages.
   - ❏ c. the rules did not work the same way for everyone.

8. One can conclude that the Olympic Organizing Committee
   - ❏ a. has held firm to its original vision of the Olympic Games.
   - ❏ b. has struggled with the definition of *amateur* over the years.
   - ❏ c. regards itself as an organization for professional athletes only.

9. The financial support given to athletes by the Soviet government can best be compared to
   - ❏ a. a gift received on a special occasion, such as a birthday.
   - ❏ b. money received from a winning lottery ticket.
   - ❏ c. an allowance paid to a child.

10. One can conclude that
    - ❏ a. the IOC's decision to allow professional athletes has supporters and detractors.
    - ❏ b. the Olympics were better when they were restricted to amateurs.
    - ❏ c. the Olympics are better today with professional athletes.

Jim Thorpe: Olympic Champion or Not?

James Francis Thorpe was born into poverty on a Sac and Fox reservation in Oklahoma. Thorpe's Native American name was Wa-tho-huck, which means "Bright Path," and after winning gold medals in the pentathlon and decathlon in the 1912 Olympics his future seemed bright indeed.

Thorpe was educated at the Carlisle Indian School, where he was twice named an All-American in football and excelled at track-and-field events as well as baseball, lacrosse, basketball, ice hockey, swimming, boxing, tennis, and archery. However, he left school for awhile to work as a farm hand. During this time, he played semiprofessional baseball—earning, some think, about two dollars per game. Many poor students played ball under false names to protect their amateur status, but Thorpe used his own name. When a reporter revealed this, the Amateur Athletic Union stripped Thorpe of his amateur status and took away his gold medals.

Thorpe went on to play major-league baseball and professional football. When he could no longer participate in sports, his life took a downward turn. He had trouble finding jobs and became an alcoholic.

Controversy over Thorpe's Olympic disqualification continued even as he was named "the best all-around athlete of the first half of the twentieth century" in 1950. In 1982 the International Olympic Committee posthumously restored Thorpe's medals.

1. **Recognizing Words in Context**

   Find the word *posthumously* in the passage. One definition below is closest to the meaning of that word. One definition has the opposite or nearly the opposite meaning. The remaining definition has a completely different meaning. Label the definitions C for *closest*, O for *opposite or nearly opposite,* and D for *different.*

   _____ a. after death

   _____ b. during life

   _____ c. angrily

2. **Distinguishing Fact from Opinion**

   Two of the statements below present *facts,* which can be proved. The other statement is an *opinion,* which expresses someone's thoughts or beliefs. Label the statements F for *fact* and O for *opinion.*

   _____ a. Thorpe was the best athlete of the first part of the twentieth century.

   _____ b. Thorpe demonstrated great athletic gifts at school.

   _____ c. Thorpe did not succeed at a new career after he retired from sports.

3. Keeping Events in Order

Number the statements below 1, 2, and 3 to show the order in which the events took place.

_____ a. Thorpe is named "best all-around athlete of the first half of the twentieth century."

_____ b. Thorpe wins a gold metal in the pentathlon and decathlon in the 1912 Olympics.

_____ c. The International Olympic Committee restores Thorpe's medals.

4. Making Correct Inferences

Two of the statements below are correct *inferences*, or reasonable guesses. They are based on information in the passage. The other statement is an incorrect, or faulty, inference. Label the statements C for *correct* inference and F for *faulty* inference.

_____ a. Thorpe depended on sports as a way to make his life better.

_____ b. Before the 1971 Olympics, student athletes were not allowed to play professional sports.

_____ c. If Thorpe had used a false name when playing semiprofessional ball, his eligibility to compete in the Olympics would never have been questioned.

5. Understanding Main Ideas

One of the statements below expresses the main idea of the passage. One statement is too general, or too broad. The other explains only part of the passage; it is too narrow. Label the statements M for *main idea*, B for *too broad*, and N for *too narrow*.

_____ a. The International Olympic Committee is responsible for solving challenging problems.

_____ b. Jim Thorpe, outstanding athlete and Olympic gold medal winner, became a victim of the controversy surrounding amateurism.

_____ c. Jim Thorpe excelled at every sport he played at the Carlisle Indian School.

Correct Answers, Part A _____

Correct Answers, Part B _____

Total Correct Answers _____

In ancient times, the Mediterranean Sea was the crossroads of civilizations, the body of water that linked the continents of Europe, Asia, and Africa. To the Greeks it was the "inner sea," as opposed to the great, uncharted "outer sea" to the west. To the Romans, it was the *Mare Nostrum,* "our sea," located at the heart of their empire. A comparatively shallow body in which the water circulates counterclockwise, the Mediterranean is famous for its violent and unpredictable storms. Scholars estimate that in ancient times some 40,000 vessels disappeared into its depths. Relics and historical records suggest that most shipwrecks occurred on the main trade routes, often near the coasts where the winds and currents are both fast and powerful.

The Phoenicians were perhaps the most expert of the early seafarers in the Mediterranean. Originally a culture in what is modern-day Lebanon on the eastern edge of the Mediterranean, Phoenicia established colonies throughout the region—in the Middle East, North Africa, Spain, and Italy. It is not known what the people called themselves, but the Greek poet Homer referred to them as "Phoenicians," a name that probably is related to the name of the brilliant red-purple dye produced from a shellfish common along the shore near the city of Tyre.

The Phoenicians were the great navigators and merchants of the ancient world and prevailed as a trading power between 1100 and 800 B.C. A Greek soldier and writer of the fifth century B.C. found the Phoenician boat a model of efficient organization, carrying equipment, supplies, and merchandise stowed neatly into spaces designed for that purpose. Sails and oars provided power; the round shape of the hull provided plenty of space for cargo; and Phoenician vessels were well-equipped to withstand the impact of waves and weather on the open sea.

Phoenicians were able to sail at night by orienting themselves to the stars. In fact, they were the first to identify Polaris, the North Star. They were secretive about their discoveries and protective of their trading partners. The Phoenicians carried lumber, perfume, textiles, and salt from the East and traded these for ivory and ebony in Africa; silver, iron, and lead in Spain; and wool, wine, and precious gems in Syria.

As a people, the Phoenicians were respected but seldom liked. Although the Hebrews of the Old Testament praised their ships made of oak and cedar, Homer, the poet who had named them, called them "greedy rogues."

Reading Time _____

Recalling Facts

1. The Greeks called the Mediterranean Sea
   - ❏ a. the "inner sea."
   - ❏ b. the *Mare Nostrum*.
   - ❏ c. the crossroads of civilization.

2. Most ancient shipwrecks occurred
   - ❏ a. off the main trade routes.
   - ❏ b. near coasts where there are strong winds and currents.
   - ❏ c. near the eastern edge of the Mediterranean.

3. The word *Phoenicia*
   - ❏ a. is a Greek word that may refer to a purple dye produced in Tyre.
   - ❏ b. describes the attitude of the Greeks toward the people of Tyre.
   - ❏ c. is another name for the North Star.

4. The Phoenicians were at their height of power
   - ❏ a. between A.D. 800 and 1100.
   - ❏ b. between 1100 and 800 B.C.
   - ❏ c. in the fifth century b.c.

5. As a people, Phoenicians were
   - ❏ a. popular but not dependable.
   - ❏ b. not very interested in science.
   - ❏ c. respected but not often liked.

Understanding Ideas

6. The Mediterranean is described as the "crossroads" of civilizations, which suggests that
   - ❏ a. the civilizations of Africa, Asia, and Europe had developed regular contact by sea.
   - ❏ b. land travel was undeveloped.
   - ❏ c. boats provided a safe way for people to travel.

7. One can infer from this passage that
   - ❏ a. a successful voyage across the Mediterranean was unusual.
   - ❏ b. it takes knowledge and skill to navigate the Mediterranean successfully.
   - ❏ c. the Phoenicians were the first to navigate the Mediterranean.

8. The Romans likely referred to the Mediterranean as "our sea" because
   - ❏ a. they would not allow other peoples to use it.
   - ❏ b. the waters were calmer near Italy.
   - ❏ c. it was integral to the Roman economy and culture.

9. One can conclude from this passage that the Phoenicians dominated trade in the Mediterranean because
   - ❏ a. they were feared by most of the other Mediterranean cultures.
   - ❏ b. they had mastered an efficient way to navigate.
   - ❏ c. they produced a popular dye.

10. Which of the following best describes a Phoenician merchant vessel?
    - ❏ a. A place for everything and everything in its place.
    - ❏ b. Appearances can be deceiving.
    - ❏ c. You get what you pay for.

Vacationing in Costa del Sol

A vacation on Spain's Costa del Sol can be a wonderful experience. The journey there is straightforward—generally a flight into Madrid and then a plane to Málaga. Málaga is the capital of the province of Andalusia. It is a prime destination on the western end of the Mediterranean.

There have been settlements along the Costa del Sol since the Phoenicians established a colony there in the eleventh century B.C. The area's geographic advantages and scenic beauty subsequently attracted the attentions of Greek merchants, Roman emperors, European monarchs, and Islamic rulers.

Marbella, one of the most fashionable resorts on the Costa del Sol, is a popular vacation stop. According to brochures, Marbella has 24 beaches spread along 17 miles of coastline. Ruins—such as Roman structures, a fifth-century Christian basilica, and a tenth-century fortress—are everywhere, and most visitors find the mix of cultures fascinating.

From Marbella travelers can visit and admire the immense Rock of Gibraltar that looms above the strait that joins the sea to the Atlantic Ocean. If it is a clear day when they visit, they can see the coast of Morocco, which is less than 10 miles away. Gibraltar, a promontory almost completely surrounded by sea, is currently a part of Great Britain, but the question of its true ownership is controversial.

1. **Recognizing Words in Context**

Find the word *promontory* in the passage. One definition below is closest to the meaning of that word. One definition has the opposite or nearly the opposite meaning. The remaining definition has a completely different meaning. Label the definitions C for *closest*, O for *opposite or nearly opposite*, and D for *different*.

_____ a. island

_____ b. peninsula

_____ c. inlet

2. **Distinguishing Fact from Opinion**

Two of the statements below present *facts*, which can be proved. The other statement is an *opinion*, which expresses someone's thoughts or beliefs. Label the statements F for *fact* and O for *opinion*.

_____ a. The Costa del Sol has attracted attention from many nations over the past 3,000 years.

_____ b. There is disagreement over which nation has control of Gibraltar.

_____ c. The Costa del Sol is a wonderful place.

3. Keeping Events in Order

Number the statements below 1, 2, and 3 to show the order in which the events took place.

_____ a. Roman emperors recognize the region's advantages.

_____ b. Spain and Great Britain disagree over the ownership of Gibraltar.

_____ c. Phoenicians colonize the Costa del Sol.

4. Making Correct Inferences

Two of the statements below are correct *inferences,* or reasonable guesses. They are based on information in the passage. The other statement is an incorrect, or faulty, inference. Label the statements C for *correct* inference and F for *faulty* inference.

_____ a. Visitors to Marbella are interested in fashion.

_____ b. The climate of the Costa del Sol is warm and pleasant.

_____ c. The controversy over control of Gibraltar is probably a result of its strategic location.

5. Understanding Main Ideas

One of the statements below expresses the main idea of the passage. One statement is too general, or too broad. The other explains only part of the passage; it is too narrow. Label the statements M for *main idea,* B for *too broad,* and N for *too narrow.*

_____ a. The Costa del Sol is famous for its beaches.

_____ b. The Mediterranean coast of Spain boasts many wonderful vacation destinations.

_____ c. The Costa del Sol is a popular resort area in Spain with a long and fascinating history.

Correct Answers, Part A _____

Correct Answers, Part B _____

Total Correct Answers _____

The Columbia River Gorge is one of the scenic wonders of the Pacific Northwest. It cuts through the Cascade mountain range, separating Washington on the north from Oregon to the south. For millennia Native American groups thrived here, taking advantage of the area's abundant fish and game. In addition to the beauty of blue waters that snake between the rock bluffs of the gorge, there are meadows bright with wildflowers, dense forests, and the white spume of waterfalls.

This paradise did not escape the notice of some people who lived in nearby cities and towns. In the early twentieth century, inspired by roads he had seen along the Rhine River valley in Europe, an Oregon lawyer named Samuel Hill began to promote his vision of a highway that would serve the community and at the same time display the area's glories. Engineer and landscape architect Samuel C. Lancaster designed a modern road that linked broad vistas with glimpses of waterfalls and leafy forest glades.

Work on the highway commenced in 1913. The road itself was built to precise requirements, with such advanced materials as reinforced concrete and new safety features such as masonry guard walls. Bridges and tunnels resembled works of art. In 1918 the Vista House, a lovely octagonal building with a copper-sheathed dome, became a popular point from which to view much of the Columbia River Gorge. In 1922 all 200 miles of concrete roadbed surfaced with asphalt opened to the public.

As automobiles became more powerful and drivers more concerned with convenience and speed than with the view through the window, Oregon's Columbia River Highway deteriorated. In the 1950s, work began on a bypass that would run straight and level on new riverbanks created from fill material dredged from the river itself. Sections of the old Columbia River Highway fell into disuse and disrepair. By the time Interstate 84 opened in 1960, the Columbia River Highway had begun to disappear.

In the 1980s, there was a resurgence of interest in the old road and the landscape around the gorge. Lost sections were identified and excavated, and a feasibility study of restoring the old Columbia River Highway to its original condition was undertaken. In 1983 surviving sections of the highway were placed on the National Register of Historic Places. The route was designated an All-American Road in 1998 and a National Historic Landmark in 2000. Preservation efforts continue to this day.

Reading Time _____

Recalling Facts

1. The Columbia River Gorge
   - ❑ a. runs alongside the Cascade Mountain Range.
   - ❑ b. is located between the states of Washington and Oregon.
   - ❑ c. is part of a valley in Europe.

2. One of the first people to envision a highway alongside the Columbia River Gorge was
   - ❑ a. a lawyer named Samuel Hill.
   - ❑ b. an architect named Samuel C. Lancaster.
   - ❑ c. a builder named Samuel Vista.

3. The Vista House
   - ❑ a. opened after the highway was complete.
   - ❑ b. offered a way to get close to a waterfall.
   - ❑ c. provided a view of much of the Columbia River Gorge.

4. The Columbia River Highway fell into disuse during the
   - ❑ a. 1920s.
   - ❑ b. 1980s.
   - ❑ c. 1950s.

5. Efforts to preserve and restore the Columbia River Highway
   - ❑ a. were initiated by Samuel Lancaster.
   - ❑ b. were undertaken in the 1980s.
   - ❑ c. have been abandoned since 2000.

Understanding Ideas

6. One can infer from this passage that the Columbia River Gorge
   - ❑ a. was not appreciated until the 1980s.
   - ❑ b. contains significant beauty.
   - ❑ c. was uninhabited until a little more than 100 years ago.

7. One can conclude that the Columbia River Highway was intended to
   - ❑ a. help people appreciate the area's natural features while also providing a transportation route.
   - ❑ b. help people travel through Oregon as quickly as possible.
   - ❑ c. make sports such as fishing and hunting more popular.

8. A drive along the Historic Columbia River Highway today will
   - ❑ a. be just like driving down the Rhine River valley in Europe.
   - ❑ b. be too rough for modern cars.
   - ❑ c. provide an experience similar to the one travelers had in 1922.

9. One can infer that the Columbia River Highway was built
   - ❑ a. to provide a safe drive.
   - ❑ b. on fill material dredged from the Columbia River.
   - ❑ c. to be a temporary solution to local transportation problems.

10. The author seems to think that
   - ❑ a. modern roads improve the whole driving experience.
   - ❑ b. many people would rather drive quickly than take time to admire the landscape along the way.
   - ❑ c. the Historic Columbia River Highway is a better road than Interstate 84.

Sister Cities: Sapporo and Portland

The sister cities of Sapporo and Portland, in Japan and Oregon, share more than a cosmopolitan outlook: Both were frontier towns in the second half of the nineteenth century and then developed into notable centers of urban life and culture.

Founded in 1845, Portland became rich through serving as a shipping port and through its lumber business. Agriculture is also important to Portland, and the area has become known for the fine wines produced there.

In 1857 Japanese people arrived on the island of Hokkaido. Sapporo was settled as a farming community and later became a producer of beer and dairy products. In the 1880s, it became a center for the export of coal. Sapporo also hosted the 1972 Winter Olympics.

Portland became Sapporo's first "sister city" in 1959. In 1986 the Sapporo Sister Cities Association was founded, and Sapporo went on to create ties to cities in Germany, China, and Russia. Portland also enlarged its family with other sister cities.

The deep tones of an immense bronze bell, a gift from Sapporo to Portland, resonate at certain times throughout the area near the Portland Convention Center. Another gift, an antique stone lantern in the form of a pagoda that arrived in 1963, was placed near the Upper Pond in Portland's Japanese Garden on stones arranged in the shape of the island of Hokkaido.

1. **Recognizing Words in Context**

   Find the word *cosmopolitan* in the passage. One definition below is closest to the meaning of that word. One definition has the opposite or nearly the opposite meaning. The remaining definition has a completely different meaning. Label the definitions C for *closest,* O for *opposite or nearly opposite,* and D for *different.*

   _____ a. sophisticated

   _____ b. chronological

   _____ c. provincial

2. **Distinguishing Fact from Opinion**

   Two of the statements below present *facts,* which can be proved. The other statement is an *opinion,* which expresses someone's thoughts or beliefs. Label the statements F for *fact* and O for *opinion.*

   _____ a. Agriculture is important to both Portland and Sapporo.

   _____ b. Every city should have a sister-city relationship.

   _____ c. Sapporo is one of Japan's newer cities.

3. Keeping Events in Order

Number the statements below 1, 2, and 3 to show the order in which the events took place.

_____ a. Sapporo is settled as a farming community.

_____ b. Sapporo founds its Sister Cities Association.

_____ c. Portland and Sapporo become sister cities.

4. Making Correct Inferences

Two of the statements below are correct *inferences,* or reasonable guesses. They are based on information in the passage. The other statement is an incorrect, or faulty, inference. Label the statements C for *correct* inference and F for *faulty* inference.

_____ a. sister-city relationships help people learn about other cultures.

_____ b. Agricultural regions tend to be wealthy.

_____ c. Sapporo viewed its sister-city relationship with Portland as a success.

5. Understanding Main Ideas

One of the statements below expresses the main idea of the passage. One statement is too general, or too broad. The other explains only part of the passage; it is too narrow. Label the statements M for *main idea,* B for *too broad,* and N for *too narrow.*

_____ a. Sister-city relationships exist between many great world cities.

_____ b. Sapporo and Portland are sister cities that also have much in common.

_____ c. Sapporo gave a bronze bell to its sister city of Portland.

Correct Answers, Part A _____

Correct Answers, Part B _____

Total Correct Answers _____

"Neither a borrower nor a lender be." Although this may well be excellent advice in matters pertaining to family and friends, borrowing and lending are frequently the foundation of a prosperous economy.

A loan is a sum of money borrowed for a limited period. A loan may be obtained from an individual or from an institution such as a bank and is generally granted at a specific rate of interest. *Interest* is the fee that the borrower pays to use the money. An extremely high rate of interest— and certainly any amount more than law permits—is called *usury*. Lending money can be a perilous business; there is always the possibility that the borrower may default on the loan. For this reason, a lender generally requires the borrower to cite an asset, known as *collateral,* as a component of the loan agreement. A house or an automobile, investments in the stock market, even the value of a business, are all examples of collateral that a lender may be willing to accept in the event that the borrower defaults on the loan.

There are two major categories of loans: consumer loans and commercial loans. A consumer loan is one that is made to an individual. It may be to buy a house or an automobile or to finance an education. A commercial loan may be used to start a new business, pay for new equipment and staff, or expand an office or factory. A mortgage—money loaned to buy or improve property—can be either a consumer or a commercial loan.

The business of making loans also contributes to a healthy economy by enhancing the employment market; mortgages allow consumers to buy and improve homes, generating work for carpenters, plumbers, and architects. New-car loans stimulate the automotive industry from the factory to the showroom, and brisk sales create jobs in industries that supply materials, from rubber and steel to computers. Loans enable businesses to expand; and when these businesses open a branch office or a new store, they also increase their consumption of office supplies, furnishings, and computers.

In a thriving economy, money circulates quickly, and each transaction represents earnings for someone. It may even be reasonable to say that a certain level of debt is normal, even necessary, to a healthy economy as long as the individual borrower or business is prudent and avoids taking on more than a manageable amount of debt.

Reading Time _____

Recalling Facts

1. When discussing a loan, *interest* is
   - ❏ a. another word for the amount borrowed from the lender.
   - ❏ b. a guarantee that the loan will be repaid.
   - ❏ c. the fee the borrower pays to use the money.

2. *Usury* is
   - ❏ a. an extremely high rate of interest on a loan.
   - ❏ b. a loan from a private individual.
   - ❏ c. a loan to a borrower who may not be able to pay it back.

3. A lending agency may require the borrower to offer *collateral*, which is
   - ❏ a. an asset that will go to the lender if the borrower defaults on the loan.
   - ❏ b. a statement to the effect that the borrower will repay the loan.
   - ❏ c. an agreement to pay a certain level of interest.

4. Loans made to businesses are called
   - ❏ a. consumer loans.
   - ❏ b. commercial loans.
   - ❏ c. mortgages.

5. A loan used for buying or improving a property is a
   - ❏ a. consumer loan.
   - ❏ b. mortgage loan.
   - ❏ c. collateral loan.

Understanding Ideas

6. One can conclude from the passage that loans
   - ❏ a. cause a dangerous level of debt.
   - ❏ b. are not likely to stimulate economic growth.
   - ❏ c. can benefit individuals other than the borrower.

7. One can infer that a bank
   - ❏ a. is limited by law to the level of interest that it may charge on a loan.
   - ❏ b. may charge as much interest on a loan as it likes.
   - ❏ c. has to charge the same amount of interest to all borrowers.

8. The author of this passage probably thinks that it is
   - ❏ a. a good idea to ask friends and family when one needs a loan.
   - ❏ b. best to go to a lending agency, such as a bank, for a loan.
   - ❏ c. probably better not to borrow money from a bank or any other lending agency.

9. It seems likely from this passage that most businesses
   - ❏ a. do not have enough cash on hand to pay for new equipment.
   - ❏ b. would prefer to be free of debt.
   - ❏ c. depend on loans to become established and to expand.

10. One might conclude that a healthy economy
    - ❏ a. keeps interest levels high.
    - ❏ b. has less debt than a poor economy has.
    - ❏ c. uses debt as a way to encourage spending.

18　B　Student Loans: Getting the Education You Want

The cost of a four-year college education is escalating daily. Current figures suggest that in 2002, a typical student will pay more than $26,000 per year at a private school and almost $12,000 at a public one and that those numbers will increase by about 6 percent per year.

Whatever the size of one's college savings account, additional sources of funds (including government grants, private scholarships, and a variety of loan programs) are available to students. The first step a student must take to find the money needed is to fill out a FAFSA form (free application for federal student aid), because all government and most private lending agencies use the information provided on it. Students can get these forms from their high school or college counselor or from the Internet.

College loans typically are granted either to the student or to the parents. Student loans—such as the Stafford Loan—are sponsored by the government and have a low interest rate. They do not have to be repaid until the student has graduated or left school. The most common loan for parents is a government-sponsored, low-interest Plus Loan, which the borrower must begin to repay immediately. Some parents also seek alternative loans and may, for example, take out a second mortgage on their home.

1. **Recognizing Words in Context**

   Find the word *escalating* in the passage. One definition below is closest to the meaning of that word. One definition has the opposite or nearly the opposite meaning. The remaining definition has a completely different meaning. Label the definitions C for *closest*, O for *opposite or nearly opposite*, and D for *different*.

   _____ a. dehydrating

   _____ b. increasing

   _____ c. plummeting

2. **Distinguishing Fact from Opinion**

   Two of the statements below present *facts*, which can be proved. The other statement is an *opinion*, which expresses someone's thoughts or beliefs. Label the statements F for *fact* and O for *opinion*.

   _____ a. Parents should take out a Plus Loan rather than a second mortgage.

   _____ b. The Stafford Loan is sponsored by the U.S. government.

   _____ c. Students often use money from several sources to pay for their educations.

3. **Keeping Events in Order**

Number the statements below 1, 2, and 3 to show the order in which the events took place.

_____ a. The college loan is paid back.

_____ b. Students fill out and file the FAFSA form.

_____ c. Parents apply for a Plus Loan.

4. **Making Correct Inferences**

Two of the statements below are correct *inferences*, or reasonable guesses. They are based on information in the passage. The other statement is an incorrect, or faulty, inference. Label the statements C for *correct* inference and F for *faulty* inference.

_____ a. It is wise to start preparing for the cost of college as far in advance as possible.

_____ b. Students who are fully enrolled in school do not need to start repayment of their Stafford loans.

_____ c. Most parents finance their children's education for college by saving the money ahead of time.

5. **Understanding Main Ideas**

One of the statements below expresses the main idea of the passage. One statement is too general, or too broad. The other explains only part of the passage; it is too narrow. Label the statements M for *main idea*, B for *too broad*, and N for *too narrow*.

_____ a. Loans are an important means of defraying the cost of an increasingly expensive college education.

_____ b. The cost of a college education is rising by about 6 percent a year.

_____ c. There are many ways to pay for a student's college education.

Correct Answers, Part A _____

Correct Answers, Part B _____

Total Correct Answers _____

The Warsaw Ghetto Uprising

A *ghetto* is a section of a city occupied by a minority, such as the former traditional residential neighborhood for Jews in Europe. The Nazis, however, transformed the ghettos into walled prisons, where starvation and disease were rampant. The German government passed its first anti-Jewish laws in 1933, and within six years it began to confine Jews to the ghettos, beginning in Poland. In 1941 the "final solution"—the methodical extermination of the Jewish people—began. Ghettos were emptied and their residents taken to concentration camps such as Treblinka, Auschwitz, and Bergen-Belsen.

At one point, the Warsaw Ghetto in Poland contained as many as 500,000 men, women, and children. The Nazis sealed it off from the rest of the city in 1940. They initially put some of its residents to work in factories making goods for the German war effort. Then, in the summer of 1942, the Nazis began to transport large groups from the ghetto to places they claimed were part of a "resettlement program." Over the next few months, as many as 300,000 Jews were deported from Warsaw, most of them to the death camp at Treblinka. By the fall of 1942, many of those who remained had decided to resist further deportations and formed the Z.O.B., whose Polish name means Jewish Combat Organization. The Z.O.B. called for a halt to cooperation with authorities and prepared for armed resistance.

On April 19, 1943, Nazi troops surrounded the Warsaw Ghetto in Poland, prepared to destroy it completely. In the ensuing battle, trained soldiers using armored vehicles, heavy artillery, and flame throwers took on members of the Jewish resistance who had a small stockpile of grenades, rifles, and pistols. As the ghetto burned down, some Jews attempted to escape through the sewers, but the Nazis filled the sewers with poison gas. On May 16, the destruction of the neighborhood's historic Tlomecki Synagogue signaled a German victory. Germany's Major General Stroop wrote his report: "The Warsaw ghetto is no more." A few hundred Nazi soldiers died in the Warsaw Ghetto uprising. It is believed that 56,000 Jews were killed during the battle, executed afterwards, or sent to die in concentration camps.

Ironically, April 19, 1943 was the first day of Passover, the Jewish holy days that commemorate the escape of the Israelites from slavery in Egypt. Few escaped from the Warsaw Ghetto, however. Indeed, only a handful of the people confined there survived World War II.

Reading Time _____

Recalling Facts

1. Warsaw is a city in
   - ❑ a. Germany.
   - ❑ b. Poland.
   - ❑ c. Bulgaria.

2. The German government passed its first anti-Jewish laws in
   - ❑ a. 1929.
   - ❑ b. 1933.
   - ❑ c. 1942.

3. Traditionally, the ghettos in Europe were the
   - ❑ a. Jewish neighborhoods.
   - ❑ b. Jewish prisons.
   - ❑ c. commercial areas of cities throughout Europe.

4. The Z.O.B. was
   - ❑ a. the name the Germans gave to the Jewish resistance.
   - ❑ b. the organization that governed Warsaw.
   - ❑ c. the Polish name for the Jewish resistance.

5. At the end of the Warsaw uprising,
   - ❑ a. Jewish survivors were sent to concentration camps.
   - ❑ b. Jewish survivors were put to work in factories in Warsaw.
   - ❑ c. the Jews rebuilt the Tlomecki Synagogue.

Understanding Ideas

6. One can conclude that the Warsaw Ghetto uprising
   - ❑ a. represented a turning point in the war.
   - ❑ b. was carried out mostly through hand-to-hand combat.
   - ❑ c. was unsuccessful for the Jewish people.

7. It seems likely that nearly
   - ❑ a. 500,000 Polish Jews died during World War II.
   - ❑ b. 500,000 Jewish people from Warsaw died at the hands of the Nazis.
   - ❑ c. 300,000 Jewish people worked in Warsaw's factories.

8. One can infer from this passage that anti-Jewish feeling in Germany
   - ❑ a. was a problem before the beginning of World War II.
   - ❑ b. became a problem only after the beginning of World War II.
   - ❑ c. ended with the implementation of the "final solution."

9. The destruction of the Tlomecki Synagogue by the Germans could probably best be described as
   - ❑ a. an act of remorse.
   - ❑ b. a heroic deed.
   - ❑ c. a symbolic gesture.

10. The irony of the uprising, which began on the first day of Passover,
    - ❑ a. is that it failed.
    - ❑ b. is that Passover celebrates the escape of the Israelites from Egypt but the uprising ended in destruction.
    - ❑ c. was a force behind the organization of the Z.O.B.

19 B Raoul Wallenberg: The Hero Who Disappeared

Raoul Wallenberg, a Swedish envoy, has been called an "angel" who saved the lives of thousands of Jews during World War II. In 1944 Wallenberg traveled to Hungary in an effort to save Jews from Nazi persecution. He designed a flashy but official-looking pass and used it to bring countless Jews out of the country. He also established some 30 "Swedish houses" in Budapest, where 15,000 refugees found sanctuary at one time or another.

For a year, Wallenberg gave out his passes, even stuffing them through the windows of trains headed to death camps. He forced Nazi officials to honor them, using threats, bribery, and the sheer force of his personality. Altogether, Wallenberg may have saved 100,000 lives. By the time the Russians arrived in Budapest in 1945, however, only 97,000 Jews were still living in the ghettos.

Wallenberg disappeared in January 1945, before World War II ended. He was on his way to Soviet headquarters in Hungary and told friends that he would be back in about eight days. In 1957 the Soviet government stated that Wallenberg had died in one of its prisons in 1947. There has never been any reasonable explanation for why he was arrested or conclusive proof of his death. Today, the circumstances surrounding his disappearance are unknown, and his whereabouts (if, indeed, he is still alive) remain a mystery.

1. **Recognizing Words in Context**

   Find the word *conclusive* in the passage. One definition below is closest to the meaning of that word. One definition has the opposite or nearly the opposite meaning. The remaining definition has a completely different meaning. Label the definitions C for *closest*, O for *opposite or nearly opposite*, and D for *different*.

   _____ a. tentative

   _____ b. hurtful

   _____ c. decisive

2. **Distinguishing Fact from Opinion**

   Two of the statements below present *facts*, which can be proved. The other statement is an *opinion*, which expresses someone's thoughts or beliefs. Label the statements F for *fact* and O for *opinion*.

   _____ a. Wallenberg was a Swedish envoy to Hungary during World War II.

   _____ b. Wallenberg had the most creative approach to helping Jews during World War II.

   _____ c. The circumstances surrounding Wallenberg's disappearance are unclear.

3. Keeping Events in Order

Number the statements below 1, 2, and 3 to show the order in which the events took place.

_____ a. Wallenberg is sent to Hungary as an envoy.

_____ b. Wallenberg provides passes that help Jews escape.

_____ c. Wallenberg travels to Soviet headquarters in Hungary.

4. Making Correct Inferences

Two of the statements below are correct *inferences*, or reasonable guesses. They are based on information in the passage. The other statement is an incorrect, or faulty, inference. Label the statements C for *correct* inference and F for *faulty* inference.

_____ a. The Soviet army was committed to rescuing Jewish people.

_____ b. The Soviet Union fought against Germany in World War II.

_____ c. Wallenberg was imaginative in his approach to rescuing Hungary's Jews.

5. Understanding Main Ideas

One of the statements below expresses the main idea of the passage. One statement is too general, or too broad. The other explains only part of the passage; it is too narrow. Label the statements M for *main idea*, B for *too broad*, and N for *too narrow*.

_____ a. Raoul Wallenberg printed passes that Jews used to escape from Hungary during the Nazi occupation.

_____ b. The Swede, Raoul Wallenberg, was clever and brave in his efforts to save Hungarian Jews.

_____ c. Heroes of World War II include Raoul Wallenberg.

Correct Answers, Part A _____

Correct Answers, Part B _____

Total Correct Answers _____

John Lackland and the Magna Carta

In 1199, upon the death of King Richard "the Lionhearted" of the Plantagenet family, his brother John ascended the throne of England. Vindictive and greedy, John was also poor. This caused his subjects, with whom he was extremely unpopular, to nickname him "John Lackland." Of all of King John's subjects, the barons—the landowners and vassals who owed their allegiance to the Crown—were the most hostile.

John's reign was ruinous for the English people. The country had been embroiled in military campaigns for decades, in part because of his desperate attempts to retain control of the Crown's possessions in France. By 1205 England had paid dearly in lives and taxes only to experience repeated defeats on the Continent while its king made other and equally powerful enemies at home. At a time when European Christians accepted the teachings of the Catholic Church in Rome, John also quarreled with the Church's leader, the Pope.

John imagined conspiracies wherever he encountered disagreement and ruled with utter disdain for English law and custom. Under these circumstances, rebellion was almost inevitable; the barons seized control of the capital city of London and battled the king's soldiers to a stalemate. In 1215, as King John traveled toward Runnymede, a meadow on the southern bank of the River Thames, his relationship with his barons was in shambles. With neither side able to claim victory, the two sides negotiated a compromise. The Magna Carta, the "Great Charter," signed at Runnymede, articulated that compromise.

The original version of the Magna Carta stipulated that rights traditional in English law for centuries be recognized. It permitted the Church to appoint its own officials without the interference of the king and obligated the king to obtain the consent of his vassals before collecting unusually large sums of money. It also reaffirmed the right of all free men charged with a crime to the protections offered by legal procedures.

King John's signature on the Magna Carta did not resolve the conflict permanently, however. John later argued that he had been forced to sign, and the Pope nullified the document. The barons revolted again, restoring the Magna Carta in 1216, after John's death. It was subsequently revised and reissued but ceased to be an influence in English law and politics before the end of the seventeenth century. The principles of justice that it defined, however, remain today.

Reading Time _____

Recalling Facts

1. King John belonged to the ruling family named
   - ❏ a. Plantagenet.
   - ❏ b. Runnymede.
   - ❏ c. Thames.

2. Which of the following is *not* true of the English barons in King John's time?
   - ❏ a. They were the country's great landowners.
   - ❏ b. They were vassals who owed their allegiance to the Crown.
   - ❏ c. The were opposed to the power of the Church.

3. King John fought in France because
   - ❏ a. he wanted to keep control of land that had belonged to England.
   - ❏ b. he had a quarrel with the Pope.
   - ❏ c. France wanted him to sign the Magna Carta.

4. The Magna Carta
   - ❏ a. was an agreement between the English Crown and the Church in Rome that articulated the King's authority.
   - ❏ b. was a document that stated the principles that had guided English law for centuries.
   - ❏ c. is considered the modern English constitution.

5. The Magna Carta provided
   - ❏ a. a temporary resolution to the conflict between the king and the barons.
   - ❏ b. long-term peace and prosperity for England.
   - ❏ c. new sources of income for the English Crown.

Understanding Ideas

6. From reading the passage, one can conclude that King John
   - ❏ a. was unfairly treated by his family.
   - ❏ b. had powerful friends among the barons.
   - ❏ c. believed that he was above the law.

7. When the writer refers to defeats on the Continent, it is clear that those battles took place in
   - ❏ a. England
   - ❏ b. France.
   - ❏ c. Runnymede.

8. Which of the following words might best describe King John's reign?
   - ❏ a. Enlightened
   - ❏ b. Ruthless
   - ❏ c. Innocuous

9. One can infer from this passage that the Magna Carta
   - ❏ a. was a milestone in English history.
   - ❏ b. articulated new ideas.
   - ❏ c. ended the abuses of power by English kings.

10. One can infer from this passage that English monarchs
    - ❏ a. did not need the cooperation of their subjects because the Magna Carta was signed.
    - ❏ b. turned to their vassals to raise the money needed to fight wars.
    - ❏ c. were always tyrants.

Wat Tyler and the English Peasants' Revolt

In 1348–1349, bubonic plague, known as the "Black Death," engulfed Europe, killing between 25 and 50 percent of the population. In England labor became scarce, and employers complained about having to pay high wages. The government enacted legislation aimed at returning wages to their preplague levels. Reduced wages and additional taxes exacerbated the discontent and anger among England's poor. In 1380, the tax on individual adults was raised to three goats; and as the government became aggressive in collecting taxes, peasant anger erupted in violence.

In 1381 a charismatic leader named Wat Tyler marched into London at the head of rioting mobs that ransacked and burned houses and demanded to see King Richard II. Little is known about Tyler except that his given name was Walter and he was a roof tiler by trade. The king met with some rebels and acceded to several demands. Nevertheless, Tyler and his followers stormed the Tower of London, capturing and executing some officials, including the lord chancellor and the royal treasurer.

The next day, at another meeting with the king, Tyler presented new demands. It seems that Tyler then came to blows with William Walworth, the mayor of London. Tyler was wounded and soon died. The uprising ended, up to 1,500 rebels were tried and hanged, and the king withdrew the promises he had made.

1. **Recognizing Words in Context**

    Find the word *exacerbated* in the passage. One definition below is closest to the meaning of that word. One definition has the opposite or nearly the opposite meaning. The remaining definition has a completely different meaning. Label the definitions C for *closest*, O for *opposite or nearly opposite,* and D for *different*.

    _____ a. stigmatized

    _____ b. intensified

    _____ c. eased

2. **Distinguishing Fact from Opinion**

    Two of the statements below present *facts,* which can be proved. The other statement is an *opinion,* which expresses someone's thoughts or beliefs. Label the statements F for *fact* and O for *opinion*.

    _____ a. Bubonic plague caused a labor shortage in England.

    _____ b. Wat Tyler was one of the rebels' leaders.

    _____ c. Wat Tyler was a charismatic leader.

3. **Keeping Events in Order**

Number the statements below 1, 2, and 3 to show the order in which the events took place.

_____ a. Rioters march into London and demand to see the king.

_____ b. Every adult is asked to pay a tax of three goats to the government.

_____ c. Bubonic plague sweeps across England.

4. **Making Correct Inferences**

Two of the statements below are correct *inferences*, or reasonable guesses. They are based on information in the passage. The other statement is an incorrect, or faulty, inference. Label the statements C for *correct* inference and F for *faulty* inference.

_____ a. Bubonic plague substantially reduced the size of England's population.

_____ b. The rebels who were executed were guilty of criminal acts.

_____ c. Taxes and low wages were not the only problems that England's peasants faced in the fourteenth century.

5. **Understanding Main Ideas**

One of the statements below expresses the main idea of the passage. One statement is too general, or too broad. The other explains only part of the passage; it is too narrow. Label the statements M for *main idea*, B for *too broad*, and N for *too narrow*.

_____ a. The Black Plague caused economic problems in England.

_____ b. Tyler died from wounds he suffered during the English Peasants' Revolt.

_____ c. Wat Tyler led a peasant revolt in England, sparked by low wages and high taxes.

Correct Answers, Part A _____

Correct Answers, Part B _____

Total Correct Answers _____

Prisons and Reform

People who are convicted of serious crimes are usually sent to prison to serve their sentences. Inmates live in small cells and are under constant surveillance by armed guards. Men and women prisoners live apart from one another and often occupy different prisons entirely.

Punishment has always been the primary purpose of prison. In the eighteenth century, wrongdoers were rarely imprisoned for extended periods of time; minor misdeeds were punished by banishment or a public whipping, and more serious acts (such as robbery, counterfeiting money, rape, and murder) were capital crimes. The punishment for a capital crime was often execution by hanging.

Reform is another reason for sentencing an offender to prison. Can an inmate learn from past mistakes, change his or her ways, and become a responsible member of society? In the nineteenth century, some people began to view prisons as agents of reform. In Pennsylvania it was widely thought that people took to crime because of negative social influences. For this reason, miscreants were put into solitary confinement, given work to do, and made to study the Bible. Those in charge assumed that in solitude an inmate would become penitent and would decide to abandon his or her life of crime. They coined the term *penitentiary* to describe such prisons.

In New York, prison officials agreed that a bad environment was the primary cause of crime, but they did not agree that isolation was the solution. Hard work and cooperation, they thought, was the key to reform. Their prisoners grew fresh produce and raised and butchered livestock for meat; they also made their own clothes and produced items that could be used or sold for profit by the state.

Generally speaking, modern prisons regard education, job training, and psychological- and substance-abuse counseling as the path to rehabilitation. Inmates can earn a high school equivalency diploma and learn new skills at jobs throughout the institution. Prerelease programs also attempt to ease an individual's return to society through visits home and other activities outside the prison.

Sadly, the prison *subculture*—the society established by the inmates—often undermines the positive effects of education programs and counseling. Many prisoners fear the power of some members of this subculture more than they do that of the prison authorities. In an environment such as this, a first-time offender may become a chronic offender and return to prison repeatedly.

Reading Time _____

Recalling Facts

1. Over the years, the main purpose of prison has been
   - ❏ a. reform.
   - ❏ b. discipline.
   - ❏ c. punishment.

2. In nineteenth-century Pennsylvania prisons, inmates were isolated from each other to
   - ❏ a. keep them safe within the prison subculture.
   - ❏ b. eliminate the bad influences it was thought caused crime.
   - ❏ c. give them time to earn a high school equivalency diploma.

3. The term *penitentiary*
   - ❏ a. was coined to suggest a place in which inmates would repent of their crimes and change their ways.
   - ❏ b. was coined by the authorities that ran the New York State prisons.
   - ❏ c. was the name given all jails in the eighteenth century.

4. Modern prison systems
   - ❏ a. place most inmates in solitary confinement.
   - ❏ b. offer education, counseling, and job training.
   - ❏ c. focus on punishment rather than reform.

5. The prison subculture
   - ❏ a. works together with prison officials to control the inmates.
   - ❏ b. is a social structure established by authorities in each prison.
   - ❏ c. often undermines the positive effects of official prison pro-grams.

Understanding Ideas

6. One can conclude that the experience of prison
   - ❏ a. is likely to deter a person from committing any new crimes.
   - ❏ b. may immerse a person into a life of crime.
   - ❏ c. is the best route to rehabilitation.

7. One can infer from this passage that
   - ❏ a. there are various views on how to rehabilitate people who have committed crimes.
   - ❏ b. there is widespread agreement on how inmates should be rehabilitated.
   - ❏ c. there are few differences between the punishment of crimes today and that in the eighteenth century.

8. It seems likely from this passage that prison reformers
   - ❏ a. understand that criminals are unlikely to become responsible members of society.
   - ❏ b. believe that a prison should do more than punish criminals.
   - ❏ c. respect the value of the subculture in the prison.

9. One might conclude that a large number of prison inmates
   - ❏ a. are well educated.
   - ❏ b. have good job skills that they can use in society.
   - ❏ c. lack a good education.

10. A chronic offender is a person who
    - ❏ a. reforms after committing a single crime.
    - ❏ b. habitually commits crimes.
    - ❏ c. suffers a long-term illness in a prison setting.

21 B   Mothers in Prison

The direct victims of crime are the people who have been injured, robbed, or murdered, yet there are other people whom one might regard as victims. Perhaps these people can more accurately be termed victims of justice.

   The children of prison inmates are one such group of victims. Between 75 and 80 percent of women inmates are mothers, and about 25 percent of those women are pregnant or have recently had a child. Statistically these children are more likely to suffer neglect or become involved with crime. As the number of women in the American prison system continues to grow, both state and federal justice systems are being challenged to address these problems. One program that has enjoyed positive results is the Mother-Infant Care (MIC) program in California.

   The MIC program was created in 1978 as an alternative to conventional imprisonment. Eligible women can be transferred from their state prison to a residential facility where they can live with their children. This highly structured program includes parenting classes, substance-abuse counseling, and other activities aimed at making positive changes in the lives of the inmates. For the children, it offers the security of a stable home and an intact family. Since 1988 pregnant women can be placed in the MIC program directly so that they need not be separated from their newborns.

1. **Recognizing Words in Context**

   Find the word *statistically* in the passage. One definition below is closest to the meaning of that word. One definition has the opposite or nearly the opposite meaning. The remaining definition has a completely different meaning. Label the definitions C for *closest*, O for *opposite or nearly opposite*, and D for *different*.

   _____ a. following state regulations

   _____ b. according to guesswork

   _____ c. according to analyzed data

2. **Distinguishing Fact from Opinion**

   Two of the statements below present *facts*, which can be proved. The other statement is an *opinion*, which expresses someone's thoughts or beliefs. Label the statements F for *fact* and O for *opinion*.

   _____ a. The number of women in prisons is increasing.

   _____ b. The children of women inmates are more victimized than children of male inmates are.

   _____ c. Children whose mothers are in prison are at higher risk of neglect.

3. **Keeping Events in Order**

   Number the statements below 1, 2, and 3 to show the order in which the events took place.

   _____ a. The MIC program is developed.

   _____ b. The State of California sees the need to address the problem of children of prison inmates.

   _____ c. Some inmates are able to live with their children after giving birth.

4. **Making Correct Inferences**

   Two of the statements below are correct *inferences*, or reasonable guesses. They are based on information in the passage. The other statement is an incorrect, or faulty, inference. Label the statements C for *correct* inference and F for *faulty* inference.

   _____ a. Crime has repercussions beyond the criminal act itself.

   _____ b. The number of women in American prisons will eventually surpass the number of men.

   _____ c. Some women in the prison system have substance-abuse problems.

5. **Understanding Main Ideas**

   One of the statements below expresses the main idea of the passage. One statement is too general, or too broad. The other explains only part of the passage; it is too narrow. Label the statements M for *main idea*, B for *too broad*, and N for *too narrow*.

   _____ a. California's MIC program includes parenting classes.

   _____ b. California's MIC program addresses the problem of women inmates and their children.

   _____ c. Incarcerating women creates additional social problems.

   Correct Answers, Part A _____

   Correct Answers, Part B _____

   Total Correct Answers _____

The Community College: Meeting the Needs of the People

The community college has been around for more than 100 years. At first community colleges were simply a continuation of high school. Students took classes in English, history, mathematics, and science that qualified them to teach children from kindergarten through the eighth grade. Small in size and responsive to demand, these colleges soon began to do more. During the Great Depression, community colleges offered job-training programs. After World War II, they helped veterans acquire the skills they would need for a peacetime economy. In the 1960s, social concerns and the search for opportunity further fueled the growth of the community-college system. Today, there are more than 1,000 such schools throughout the United States, and more than nine million people enroll in certification or degree programs each year. An additional five million people take classes to learn skills that they can use on the job or to pursue a personal interest.

Although all community colleges share a common belief in the value of continuing education, each is a unique institution that serves the needs of its community. Colleges often work with businesses to encourage economic growth. Together, they identify the skills needed in the modern workplace so that the college can design successful programs. Students can earn an associate's degree in two years or less. Community colleges also cost less to attend than a four-year university.

In rural parts of the United States, community colleges have begun to change a harsh present into a hopeful future. Steady declines in farming, mining, and forestry have resulted in high levels of unemployment and severe poverty. Young people leave their homes to try to find work in the cities. Widespread illiteracy is also a problem. In response the colleges have opened their doors to civic groups and have provided access to computers. Faculty members advise new businesses and contribute to the shaping of public policy.

Rural community colleges are also pioneers in education. They have been exploring the use of satellite television to connect teachers to students often hundreds of miles apart. Some of them, especially those affiliated with Native American communities, have also become the guardians of culture. They are centers of scholarly research and the headquarters of oral history. They preserve native arts and history and teach these subjects in the classroom. In some locations, they have even been able to link economic improvement to regional identity through cultural tourism.

Reading Time _____

Recalling Facts

1. Early community colleges
   - ❏ a. focused on social concerns and the search for opportunity.
   - ❏ b. trained people to teach children through eighth grade.
   - ❏ c. used satellite television to reach distant students.

2. Since the 1930s, community colleges
   - ❏ a. have also offered job-training programs.
   - ❏ b. have focused on foreign languages.
   - ❏ c. have become less important in higher education.

3. Students can earn an associate's degree at a community college
   - ❏ a. in four years.
   - ❏ b. in six years.
   - ❏ c. in two years or less.

4. Many rural community colleges use satellite television
   - ❏ a. to connect teachers to students who may be hundreds of miles away from one another.
   - ❏ b. to overcome local cultural traditions.
   - ❏ c. because people in many rural communities need remedial courses.

5. Because of their role as educators, some rural community colleges
   - ❏ a. are unwilling to become involved in politics or shaping public policy.
   - ❏ b. are not accustomed to dealing with older students.
   - ❏ c. have become guardians of regional culture.

Understanding Ideas

6. One can conclude from the passage that continuing education
   - ❏ a. is a form of entertainment.
   - ❏ b. focuses on new skills necessary in a changing workplace.
   - ❏ c. is a cure for widespread illiteracy.

7. In areas where jobs in farming and mining have disappeared,
   - ❏ a. people have to move away.
   - ❏ b. community colleges focus on reviving those jobs.
   - ❏ c. community colleges are helping to create new jobs.

8. Rural community colleges are looking into the use of satellite television in teaching because
   - ❏ a. people like to watch television.
   - ❏ b. many people live far away from the campus.
   - ❏ c. it delivers more effective instruction than attended classes do.

9. People might choose to attend a community college because
   - ❏ a. they lack the time or the money to enroll in a four-year college.
   - ❏ b. it offers a more intensive education than a four-year college.
   - ❏ c. it gives them a chance to live away from home.

10. Which of the following sentences is a good example of the main idea?
    - ❏ a. Rural community colleges use satellite television to connect teachers to students.
    - ❏ b. Community colleges offer low-cost education that is accessible and focused on local needs.
    - ❏ c. Community colleges are part of the public education system.

Technology and Distance Learning in Higher Education

Community colleges seek to provide vocational training for people in search of new or better jobs. Although brick-and-mortar classrooms play a part in this mission, technology is becoming more and more important.

Some colleges use television to reach those who are living in rural areas or are confined to their homes. St. Louis Community College (SLCC) in Missouri, for example, offers 15 televised courses that range from science and psychology to foreign language. Thirty years ago, it offered only a single history course.

Distance learning takes place on the campuses as well. "Teleclasses" are beamed into classrooms at different locations. Students can question the teacher or respond to comments made by "classmates" miles away. Teleclasses broaden the choice of classes for students and permit savings on salaries and other costs for the college.

Improvements in the Internet have also been a factor in the increase in distance-learning classes. An award-winning program at SLCC offers English Composition over the computer. A Web site, e-mail access, and other features promote exchanges between students and between students and teachers. Courses on the Internet, however, require costly computer equipment that may be beyond the means of many who depend on the community college for further education.

1. **Recognizing Words in Context**

   Find the word *vocational* in the passage. One definition below is closest to the meaning of that word. One definition has the opposite or nearly the opposite meaning. The remaining definition has a completely different meaning. Label the definitions C for *closest,* O for *opposite or nearly opposite,* and D for *different.*

   _____ a. recreational

   _____ b conditional

   _____ c. occupational

2. **Distinguishing Fact from Opinion**

   Two of the statements below present *facts,* which can be proved. The other statement is an *opinion,* which expresses someone's thoughts or beliefs. Label the statements F for *fact* and O for *opinion.*

   _____ a. A college-educated person can get a better job.

   _____ b. The Internet gives colleges a way to reach students in their homes.

   _____ c. Teleclasses allow students on different campuses to question the instructor or respond to comments.

3. Keeping Events in Order

Number the statements below 1, 2, and 3 to show the order in which the events took place.

_____ a. A range of courses in psychology, foreign language, and science are offered at St. Louis Community College.

_____ b A single history course is offered at St. Louis Community College.

_____ c. Award-winning courses are offered over the Internet at St. Louis Community College.

4. Making Correct Inferences

Two of the statements below are correct *inferences,* or reasonable guesses. They are based on information in the passage. The other statement is an incorrect, or faulty, inference. Label the statements C for *correct* inference and F for *faulty* inference.

_____ a. New technologies provide greater access to community-college courses.

_____ b. There are costs as well as savings with distance-learning programs.

_____ c. Distance learning makes courses at the community college available to everyone.

5. Understanding Main Ideas

One of the statements below expresses the main idea of the passage. One statement is too general, or too broad. The other explains only part of the passage; it is too narrow. Label the statements M for *main idea,* B for *too broad,* and N for *too narrow.*

_____ a. Many people throughout the country are educated at community colleges.

_____ b. Some distance-learning classes can be taught over the Internet.

_____ c. New technologies have allowed community colleges to reach more students through distance learning.

Correct Answers, Part A _____

Correct Answers, Part B _____

Total Correct Answers _____

The Maori of New Zealand

The Maori migrated to New Zealand from the islands of Polynesia to the east between 950 and 1200. The first settlements, or *kainga,* grew up along the coastline, where the people fished and hunted fur seals, dolphins, and pilot whales. The Maori cleared forests for timber, and they cultivated kumara, a kind of sweet potato, for food. Later on, these small villages expanded into larger, fortlike communities, called *pa*s, that were surrounded by fences for protection.

Maori legend holds that the people left their ancestral homes in a fleet of great canoes. This story may or may not be true, but the Maori word *waka* means both "canoe" and "a tribal group" descended from the occupants of one of the original canoes. Theirs was a highly organized society structured around family groups, tribal connections, and well-defined roles. Maori men hunted and plowed; women tended the crops, wove fabrics, and cooked. Eldest sons inherited the property, following the rules of primogeniture. The same laws controlled the succession of leaders. The arts, including poetry and oratory, were highly valued, and communal buildings featured ornamental carvings. Personal decoration, from tattoos to jewelry, was also important.

The Maori were quick to go to war, and battles between tribes are a prominent feature of their history. The first European encounter with the Maori turned bloody when four sailors from Dutch navigator Abel Tasman's ship were killed in 1642. When British explorer James Cook arrived in 1769, however, he was able to forge fairly peaceful relations. By the nineteenth century, the Maori had learned a great deal from their interaction with Europeans who made stops at New Zealand's harbors. They learned European languages and how to read and write. They also learned to use European guns. New Zealand became a British colony in 1841, and the Maori became British citizens. Subsequent disputes over the land led to a series of wars, and in the aftermath much of the remaining Maori territory was confiscated. Both wars and imported diseases, such as influenza and measles, dramatically diminished the population.

Today, racial tensions and cultural conflict still exist between the Maori and the descendents of the British who settled in New Zealand. The Maori continue their efforts to regain ancestral lands and create some form of self-rule. In 1995 the British government promised to provide compensation to the Maori for more than a century and a half of economic and social inequities.

Reading Time _____

Recalling Facts

1. The Maori of New Zealand emigrated there from
   - ❏ a. Polynesia.
   - ❏ b. Great Britain.
   - ❏ c. Holland.

2. The Maori word that refers to both a canoe and a tribal group is
   - ❏ a. kainga.
   - ❏ b. kumara.
   - ❏ c. waka.

3. Maori society was
   - ❏ a. peaceful, and members were enthusiastic about trade with Europe.
   - ❏ b. warlike, and members performed in well-defined roles.
   - ❏ c. primitive, and members placed little value on artistic work.

4. European ships
   - ❏ a. were rarely seen in New Zealand before the nineteenth century.
   - ❏ b. brought diseases, such as measles, that killed many Maori.
   - ❏ c. encountered a warm welcome from the Maori.

5. Today relations between the Maori and descendents of the British colonists
   - ❏ a. often suffer from racial tensions and cultural conflict.
   - ❏ b. have eased since the Maori became British citizens.
   - ❏ c. are usually mutually respectful.

Understanding Ideas

6. One can infer from this passage that
   - ❏ a. men and women shared the same responsibilities in traditional Maori society.
   - ❏ b. Maori girls were left poor, because only boys could inherit property.
   - ❏ c. the leaders of the Maori people were almost always male.

7. It is most likely that the *pa* style of village building evolved to protect the tribes from attacks by
   - ❏ a. European settlers.
   - ❏ b. other tribal groups.
   - ❏ c. wild animals.

8. One might infer that
   - ❏ a. there are fewer Maori today than there were before the arrival of Europeans.
   - ❏ b. the Maori have thrived culturally as citizens of Great Britain.
   - ❏ c. The Dutch claim to New Zealand was better than that of the British.

9. One might expect Maori culture to
   - ❏ a. reflect a strong Dutch influence.
   - ❏ b. include little of artistic merit.
   - ❏ c. share features with some Polynesian cultures.

10. In a society where primogeniture is the rule,
    - ❏ a. the firstborn child inherits all family wealth.
    - ❏ b. the oldest son makes sure that wealth is shared equally among his brothers and sisters.
    - ❏ c. the oldest surviving son inherits all family wealth.

Music of the Maori

Contemporary Maori music is diverse. It uses modern instruments, such as the guitar and ukulele, and incorporates such influences as classical orchestral compositions and American popular music. Before European contact, however, Maori music—from laments and lullabies to incantations and battle calls—employed only indigenous instruments, now categorized as idiophones and aerophones.

Idiophones are percussion instruments. They can be large, as is the *pahuu,* a flat slab of wood suspended in the air that resonates when struck. The pahuu was used to summon villagers in case of danger. Some pahuu take the form of a cylinder carved from a hollow tree. *Tokere,* on the other hand, are fragments of bone or shell held between the thumb and forefinger and clattered together.

Aerophones depend on air to produce sound and therefore are similar to flutes or trumpets. Flute-type instruments include the *koauau,* which are carved from pieces of bone or wood five or six inches long and have several finger holes that are used to change the sound's pitch. Maori "trumpets" are collectively described as *pu.* They functioned at first as signals or alarms, to announce the arrival of some dignitary or to alert villagers to danger. These include the *putatara,* a conch shell to which a wooden mouthpiece has been added; the larger the shell the deeper the sound it makes.

1. **Recognizing Words in Context**

   Find the word *dignitary* in the passage. One definition below is closest to the meaning of that word. One definition has the opposite or nearly the opposite meaning. The remaining definition has a completely different meaning. Label the definitions C for *closest,* O for *opposite or nearly opposite,* and D for *different.*

   _____ a. official

   _____ b. explorer

   _____ c. commoner

2. **Distinguishing Fact from Opinion**

   Two of the statements below present *facts,* which can be proved. The other statement is an *opinion,* which expresses someone's thoughts or beliefs. Label the statements F for *fact* and O for *opinion.*

   _____ a. Contemporary Maori music combines influences from American pop music with traditional forms.

   _____ b. Maori flutes are usually carved from wood or bone.

   _____ c. The sound of a pahuu is inferior to sounds such as that of a gong.

3. Keeping Events in Order

Number the statements below 1, 2, and 3 to show the order in which the events took place.

_____ a. The Maori use and carve idiophones and aerophones.

_____ b. The Maori use the ukulele.

_____ c. The Maori encounter Europeans.

4. Making Correct Inferences

Two of the statements below are correct *inferences,* or reasonable guesses. They are based on information in the passage. The other statement is an incorrect, or faulty, inference. Label the statements C for *correct* inference and F for *faulty* inference.

_____ a. Maori instruments provide a limited range of sounds.

_____ b. The Maori made musical instruments from materials they found in nature.

_____ c. Idiophones are similar to modern drums and cymbals.

5. Understanding Main Ideas

One of the statements below expresses the main idea of the passage. One statement is too general, or too broad. The other explains only part of the passage; it is too narrow. Label the statements M for *main idea,* B for *too broad,* and N for *too narrow.*

_____ a. Before contact with Europeans, the Maori invented unique musical instruments to accompany their songs and signal the villagers.

_____ b. The Maori are a musical people.

_____ c. Contemporary Maori music makes use of the guitar.

Correct Answers, Part A _____

Correct Answers, Part B _____

Total Correct Answers _____

Americans and Their Cars

The automobile may not be synonymous with modern American culture, but it has occupied a central role in America's economic and social history.

When the first Ford Model T rolled off the assembly line in 1908, businessman Henry Ford transformed the car from a luxury accessory for the rich to an affordable product for the middle classes. The rush of cars into the community forced all levels of government to build new and better roads. Better roads fed the demand for larger, faster, more stylish vehicles, and a host of companies rushed to meet that demand.

If there was a first Golden Age of the automobile, it may well have been the 1950s. Manufacturers focused on glamor, and cars got bigger. They were also more powerful and loaded with gadgets and shiny chrome. It was an age of prosperity; and large, regular paychecks encouraged the public display of wealth through costly items such as new cars. Americans, moreover, needed those cars as they moved away from the cities into the suburbs, where such things as stores, jobs, and schools were seldom within walking distance. Cars became essential if people were to get to work or to the grocery store. Leisure places, such as drive-in movies and drive-through restaurants, kept Americans in their cars.

As the 1950s slipped into the 1960s, it became apparent that these fashionable wheels were gas-guzzling road cruisers, dangerous in an accident, and often full of defects. Under pressure from a variety of groups, the federal government required that newer models provide greater fuel efficiency and cleaner emissions. Seatbelts became standard equipment as well. Spiraling fuel prices in the 1970s, coupled with concern for the environment, made the smaller cars produced by foreign companies for European and Asian markets very popular.

The 1980s and 1990s saw an upswing in the popularity of big cars. New models—including minivans and sport utility vehicles—have become staples in auto dealers' showrooms. Gridlock on the roads has become part of the American way of life. In 1911 a horse and buggy could travel through rush-hour traffic in Los Angeles at 11 miles per hour. In 2000 a car covering the same territory at the same time of day moved at about four miles per hour. But perhaps that is not important. When a car is equipped with a telephone and television set, a computer, and global positioning satellite connections, it can feel just like home.

Reading Time _____

Recalling Facts

1. Henry Ford
   - ❏ a. invented the first automobile.
   - ❏ b. transformed the car from a luxury accessory into an affordable commodity.
   - ❏ c. encouraged people to buy cars that kept getting bigger and more powerful.

2. The first Golden Age of the automobile may have been
   - ❏ a. the 1910s
   - ❏ b. the 1970s
   - ❏ c. the 1950s.

3. Cars in the 1950s turned out to be
   - ❏ a. fuel-efficient vehicles with clean emissions.
   - ❏ b. gas guzzlers that were dangerous in an accident.
   - ❏ c. better-quality cars than those imported from Europe and Asia.

4. In the 1960s, the government
   - ❏ a. required new cars to be more fuel efficient.
   - ❏ b. promoted the purchase of larger luxury cars.
   - ❏ c. eased requirements for cleaner emissions.

5. In recent decades, large vehicles
   - ❏ a. have been ignored in favor of small, fuel-efficient cars.
   - ❏ b. have come back into popularity.
   - ❏ c. have often been forced to move more slowly than a horse and buggy.

Understanding Ideas

6. One can infer from this passage that Henry Ford's Model T
   - ❏ a. was less expensive to produce than other cars of its time.
   - ❏ b. was a large, fast, and stylish vehicle.
   - ❏ c. was useless without a network of good roads.

7. One can conclude from this passage that car sales in the 1950s
   - ❏ a. fell because the newer models cars were often full of defects.
   - ❏ b. rose because many people moved to the suburbs.
   - ❏ c. rose because the cars became less expensive.

8. It seems likely that Americans developed a preference for small cars
   - ❏ a. because they started having smaller families.
   - ❏ b. when they learned that large cars were unsafe.
   - ❏ c. after the cost of gasoline rose.

9. The author might agree that gridlock
   - ❏ a. is a sign that Americans should use their cars less if they can.
   - ❏ b. is good because it gives the driver a chance to use the telephone or watch television.
   - ❏ c. proves the superiority of horses and walking as forms of transportation.

10. It would seem that today's cars
    - ❏ a. are focused on safety rather than luxury.
    - ❏ b. are less useful than a horse and buggy.
    - ❏ c. offer distractions from traffic congestion.

Route 66: The Main Street of America

Some places take on a mythic quality, entering the lore of a culture and becoming legendary. Route 66, the first highway to link Chicago to Los Angeles, has such a legendary place in American lore.

Unlike roads that went directly west and over the high passes of the Rocky Mountains, Route 66 cut a diagonal course southwest. It crossed flat prairie lands and offered mild temperatures and more dependable weather than comparable roads. Thus it became a favorite road of truck drivers and travelers, linking communities along its way that in turn gave the road its distinctive character.

In the early 1960s, a television program, *Route 66*, gave this highway a special position in the American imagination. For four seasons, viewers watched Tod and Buzz travel down its twists and turns in search of adventure. The ordinary people and eccentric personalities they met along the way seemed to personify the country in all its diversity.

Eventually, the need for speed and efficiency spelled doom for that unique road. As new superhighways were constructed, parts of the original Route 66 fell into disuse and then disrepair. It finally disappeared. In 1984 Interstate 40 in Arizona replaced the last segment of the road sometimes called the "Main Street of America." Today signposts proclaiming "Historic Route 66" are found alongside the roads that replaced it.

1. Recognizing Words in Context

Find the word *personify* in the passage. One definition below is closest to the meaning of that word. One definition has the opposite or nearly the opposite meaning. The remaining definition has a completely different meaning. Label the definitions C for *closest*, O for *opposite or nearly opposite*, and D for *different*.

_____ a. not be representative of

_____ b be symbolic of

_____ c. rotate around

2. Distinguishing Fact from Opinion

Two of the statements below present *facts*, which can be proved. The other statement is an *opinion*, which expresses someone's thoughts or beliefs. Label the statements F for *fact* and O for *opinion*.

_____ a. When it was built, Route 66 offered the traveler more dependable weather than comparable roads.

_____ b. Route 66 is one of the best highways ever constructed.

_____ c. Route 66 was eventually replaced by superhighways.

3. Keeping Events in Order

Number the statements below 1, 2, and 3 to show the order in which the events took place.

_____ a. In Arizona, Route 66 is replaced by Interstate 40.

_____ b. Route 66 links together cities and small towns between Chicago and Los Angeles.

_____ c. "Route 66" is a popular show on American television.

4. Making Correct Inferences

Two of the statements below are correct *inferences,* or reasonable guesses. They are based on information in the passage. The other statement is an incorrect, or faulty, inference. Label the statements C for *correct* inference and F for *faulty* inference.

_____ a. The weather along Route 66 was milder because the highway stayed on flat countryside rather than going over mountains.

_____ b. Older roads may be abandoned when new and faster highways are built.

_____ c. Route 66 was the best route west.

5. Understanding Main Ideas

One of the statements below expresses the main idea of the passage. One statement is too general, or too broad. The other explains only part of the passage; it is too narrow. Label the statements M for *main idea,* B for *too broad,* and N for *too narrow.*

_____ a. Route 66 inspired a television program of the same name.

_____ b. Route 66 linked Chicago and Los Angeles and holds a special place in the American imagination.

_____ c. Route 66 was one of many great modern highways.

Correct Answers, Part A _____

Correct Answers, Part B _____

Total Correct Answers _____

25 A Senator Joseph McCarthy's Crusade Against the "Red Menace"

"Are you now or have you ever been a member of the Communist Party?" This question was asked repeatedly during Senator Joseph McCarthy's relentless hunt for the Communists he believed had infiltrated every aspect of American life by the 1950s. McCarthy, a Republican, won a Senate seat in Wisconsin in 1946 and gained quick attention from the media for his provocative claims. He also incurred the hostility of his Senate colleagues when he ignored the customs and written rules of the upper chamber.

McCarthy's name became a household word following a speech in West Virginia in 1950. In this speech, he claimed that the State Department and other agencies were riddled with Communists. He waved a piece of paper on which he said were written the names of 205 Communists who held jobs in the U.S. government. This was the beginning of the period now called the McCarthy era, during which panic over the "Red menace" was pushed to new heights.

The election in 1952 brought in both a Republican president and congressional majority. McCarthy took advantage of his party's power to pursue his agenda with single-minded concentration. As chairman of the Permanent Subcommittee of Investigations, he launched a search for suspected Communists. Among his first targets was the State Department's information program, including its overseas libraries and the *Voice of America* radio broadcasts.

The hearings took a toll on those subjected to his committee's scrutiny. Famous authors and screenwriters were grilled about their beliefs, their activities, and their friends—in public and private. Many found it difficult or impossible to get their work published afterward. Members of Hollywood's film industry suffered similar problems, as McCarthy placed numerous people in the State Department under a cloud of suspicion. Many saw their careers ruined, and others had to deal with a department in disarray.

In 1954 McCarthy set his sights on the U.S. Army and began a series of televised hearings. His attacks on respected military officers and the law firm representing the Army proved to be more than the country could take. Public approval of McCarthy's search for Communists quickly turned into disapproval. Late that year, the Senate censured McCarthy for his conduct in the Senate and the tactics he used in his investigations and hearings.

Few who had been accused at the hearings were ever proved to be Communists. McCarthy died in 1957, before the end of his second term.

Reading Time _____

Recalling Facts

1. Joseph McCarthy was
   - ❑ a. a long-term senator from Wisconsin in 1946.
   - ❑ b. elected senator from Wisconsin in 1946.
   - ❑ c. a member of the Democratic Party in 1946.

2. Sen. McCarthy was intent on
   - ❑ a. identifying Communists in the United States.
   - ❑ b. infiltrating the American Communist Party.
   - ❑ c. securing positions in the U.S. government for Communists.

3. McCarthy achieved the power to pursue his agenda
   - ❑ a. when he was elected senator in 1946.
   - ❑ b. because of his speech in West Virginia in 1950.
   - ❑ c. when the Republicans became the majority party after the 1952 election.

4. McCarthy focused his attention first on
   - ❑ a. the House of Representatives.
   - ❑ b. the State Department.
   - ❑ c. the upper chamber.

5. Being called to testify at McCarthy's hearings
   - ❑ a. could result in damage to a person's career.
   - ❑ b. was a sign that a person had achieved prominence in his or her career.
   - ❑ c. was of concern primarily to writers.

Understanding Ideas

6. One can conclude that the term "Red menace" was
   - ❑ a. coined by Joseph McCarthy.
   - ❑ b. a nickname for the Republican Party.
   - ❑ c. used to describe the Communist Party.

7. One can infer that during the 1950s
   - ❑ a. most Americans rejected McCarthy's concerns about Communism.
   - ❑ b. the U.S. government was riddled with Communists.
   - ❑ c. many Americans were afraid of the spread of Communism.

8. One can infer from this passage that
   - ❑ a. McCarthy accused only those people that he could prove were Communists.
   - ❑ b. McCarthy was convinced that Communism was a threat to the country.
   - ❑ c. McCarthy's hearings were respected by his colleagues.

9. McCarthy might best be described as
   - ❑ a. obsessed by anti-Communist concerns.
   - ❑ b. a man who respected the traditions of the U.S. Senate.
   - ❑ c. a Republican who earned the respect of his colleagues.

10. Most people called to testify before McCarthy's committee probably
    - ❑ a. felt confident that they would be treated with respect.
    - ❑ b. would have liked receiving recognition in their fields.
    - ❑ c. were skeptical about being treated impartially.

Senator Margaret Chase Smith's "Declaration of Conscience"

In 1950 Wisconsin senator Joseph McCarthy and his anti-Communist crusade exploded into the news after he made sweeping accusations in a speech in West Virginia. Many were outraged by his claims and his lack of evidence, but few dared voice their concerns. Five months later, another senator finally took him to task.

Margaret Chase Smith of Maine had served four terms in the House of Representatives before going to the Senate in 1948. On June 1, 1950, she addressed the Senate, denouncing McCarthy's tactics without ever mentioning him by name. In her speech, "A Declaration of Conscience," she reproached senators who would sully the names and reputations of citizens whose political or cultural views differed from theirs. She condemned any suppression of freedom guaranteed by the U.S. Constitution. Six other senators endorsed this remarkable declaration.

McCarthy listened as Smith spoke; later he refused to comment on the speech, saying, "I don't fight with women senators." He later privately referred to Smith and the senators who had endorsed her remarks as "Snow White and her six dwarfs."

The speech made no immediate impact on McCarthy or the general climate of suspicion that had the country in its grip. Smith's speech, however, remains one of the greatest expressions of American rights ever voiced.

1. **Recognizing Words in Context**

   Find the word *indiscriminate* in the passage. One definition below is closest to the meaning of that word. One definition has the opposite or nearly the opposite meaning. The remaining definition has a completely different meaning. Label the definitions C for *closest*, O for *opposite or nearly opposite*, and D for *different*.

   _____ a. glorious

   _____ b. reasoned

   _____ c. careless

2. **Distinguishing Fact from Opinion**

   Two of the statements below present *facts*, which can be proved. The other statement is an *opinion*, which expresses someone's thoughts or beliefs. Label the statements F for *fact* and O for *opinion*.

   _____ a. Smith's speech was one of the greatest expressions of American rights.

   _____ b. McCarthy's speech in West Virginia outraged many people.

   _____ c. McCarthy paid little attention to Smith's speech.

3. Keeping Events in Order

Number the statements below 1, 2, and 3 to show the order in which the events took place.

_____ a. Smith presents "A Declaration of Conscience" in the Senate.

_____ b. McCarthy says that he "does not fight with women senators."

_____ c. McCarthy delivers an anti-Communist speech in West Virginia.

4. Making Correct Inferences

Two of the statements below are correct *inferences,* or reasonable guesses. They are based on information in the passage. The other statement is an incorrect, or faulty, inference. Label the statements C for *correct* inference and F for *faulty* inference.

_____ a. The people who heard Smith's speech understood that she was talking about McCarthy.

_____ b. Smith was an experienced politician and legislator.

_____ c. Smith was not concerned about the spread of Communism.

5. Understanding Main Ideas

One of the statements below expresses the main idea of the passage. One statement is too general, or too broad. The other explains only part of the passage; it is too narrow. Label the statements M for *main idea,* B for *too broad,* and N for *too narrow.*

_____ a. Margaret Chase Smith was a senator from Maine.

_____ b. Smith's "Declaration" condemned McCarthy's anti-Communist crusade.

_____ c. Senator Smith of Maine gave "A Declaration of Conscience" in June 1950.

Correct Answers, Part A _____

Correct Answers, Part B _____

Total Correct Answers _____

ANSWER KEY

READING RATE GRAPH

COMPREHENSION SCORE GRAPH

COMPREHENSION SKILLS PROFILE GRAPH

ANSWER KEY

1A   1. c   2. a   3. b   4. a   5. b   6. c   7. b   8. c   9. a   10. c

1B   1. O, C, D   2. F, F, O   3. S, B, S   4. C, F, C   5. B, M, N

2A   1. b   2. c   3. a   4. c   5. b   6. a   7. b   8. c   9. c   10. b

2B   1. D, C, O   2. F, O, F   3. 3, 1, 2   4. C, C, F   5. M, B, N

3A   1. c   2. a   3. b   4. b   5. b   6. b   7. a   8. c   9. b   10. c

3B   1. C, O, D   2. O, F, F   3. 1, 3, 2   4. F, C, C   5. N, B, M

4A   1. a   2. c   3. b   4. a   5. b   6. c   7. a   8. c   9. c   10. a

4B   1. O, D, C   2. F, F, O   3. 2, 1, 3   4. F, C, C   5. M, N, B

5A   1. b   2. c   3. a   4. a   5. c   6. b   7. a   8. b   9. c   10. b

5B   1. C, D, O   2. F, O, F   3. 2, 3, 1   4. C, C, F   5. B, M, N

6A   1. c   2. b   3. a   4. a   5. b   6. a   7. c   8. a   9. b   10. b

6B   1. D, O, C   2. O, F, F   3. 1, 3, 2   4. C, F, C   5. B, M, N

7A   1. b   2. c   3. a   4. b   5. c   6. a   7. c   8. b   9. c   10. b

7B   1. O, D, C   2. F, O, F   3. 3, 1, 2   4. C, C, F   5. N, M, B

8A   1. a   2. c   3. b   4. a   5. c   6. a   7. a   8. b   9. c   10. b

8B   1. C, O, D   2. F, F, O   3. 2, 3, 1   4. F, C, C   5. B, N, M

9A   1. b   2. a   3. c   4. a   5. c   6. b   7. c   8. a   9. a   10. b

9B   1. D, C, O   2. O, F, F   3. 3, 2, 1   4. C, F, C   5. M, B, N

10A   1. c   2. b   3. a   4. c   5. b   6. a   7. b   8. a   9. b   10. a

10B   1. O, C, D   2. F, O, F   3. 2, 1, 3   4. C, C, F   5. N, B, M

11A   1. b   2. b   3. c   4. a   5. c   6. c   7. b   8. a   9. b   10. c

11B   1. D, O, C   2. F, F, O   3. 3, 2, 1   4. F, C, C   5. B, M, N

12A   1. a   2. b   3. a   4. c   5. b   6. c   7. a   8. c   9. b   10. c

12B   1. C, O, D   2. F, O, F   3. 1, 3, 2   4. F, C, C   5. M, N, B

13A   1. c   2. a   3. c   4. b   5. b   6. a   7. c   8. c   9. a   10. b

13B   1. O, D, C   2. F, O, F   3. 3, 1, 2   4. C, F, C   5. N, M, B

14A	1. b	2. a	3. c	4. c	5. b	6. a	7. b	8. c	9. b	10. a
14B	1. D, C, O	2. O, F, F	3. 3, 1, 2	4. C, F, C	5. M, B, N				
15A	1. c	2. b	3. c	4. a	5. b	6. a	7. c	8. b	9. c	10. A
15B	1. C, O, D	2. O, F, F	3. 2, 1, 3	4. C, C, F	5. B, M, N				
16A	1. a	2. b	3. a	4. b	5. c	6. a	7. b	8. c	9. b	10. a
16B	1. D, C, O	2. F, F, O	3. 2, 3, 1	4. F, C, C	5. N, B, M				
17A	1. b	2. a	3. c	4. c	5. b	6. b	7. a	8. c	9. a	10. b
17B	1. C, D, O	2. F, O, F	3. 1, 3, 2	4. C, F, C	5. B, M, N				
18A	1. c	2. a	3. a	4. b	5. b	6. c	7. a	8. b	9. c	10. c
18B	1. D, C, O	2. O, F, F	3. 3, 1, 2	4. C, C, F	5. M, N, B				
19A	1. b	2. b	3. a	4. c	5. a	6. c	7. b	8. a	9. c	10. b
19B	1. O, D, C	2. F, O, F	3. 1, 2, 3	4. F, C, C	5. N, M, B				
20A	1. a	2. c	3. a	4. b	5. a	6. c	7. b	8. b	9. a	10. b
20B	1. D, C, O	2. F, F, O	3. 3, 2, 1	4. C, F, C	5. B, N, M				
21A	1. c	2. b	3. a	4. b	5. c	6. b	7. a	8. b	9. c	10. b
21B	1. D, O, C	2. F, O, F	3. 2, 1, 3	4. C, F, C	5. N, M, B				
22A	1. b	2. a	3. c	4. a	5. c	6. b	7. c	8. b	9. a	10. b
22B	1. O, D, C	2. O, F, F	3. 2, 1, 3	4. C, C, F	5. B, N, M				
23A	1. a	2. c	3. b	4. b	5. a	6. c	7. b	8. a	9. c	10. c
23B	1. C, D, O	2. F, F, O	3. 1, 3, 2	4. F, C, C	5. M, B, N				
24A	1. b	2. c	3. b	4. a	5. b	6. a	7. b	8. c	9. a	10. c
24B	1. O, C, D	2. F, O, F	3. 3, 1, 2	4. C, C, F	5. N, M, B				
25A	1. b	2. a	3. c	4. b	5. a	6. c	7. c	8. b	9. a	10. c
25B	1. D, O, C	2. O, F, F	3. 2, 3, 1	4. C, C, F	5. B, M N				

READING RATE

Put an X on the line above each lesson number to show your reading time and words-per-minute rate for that lesson.

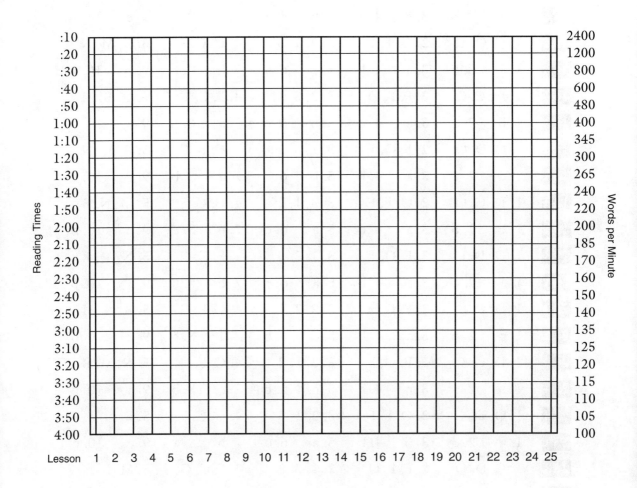

Reading Times

	Words per Minute
:10	2400
:20	1200
:30	800
:40	600
:50	480
1:00	400
1:10	345
1:20	300
1:30	265
1:40	240
1:50	220
2:00	200
2:10	185
2:20	170
2:30	160
2:40	150
2:50	140
3:00	135
3:10	125
3:20	120
3:30	115
3:40	110
3:50	105
4:00	100

Lesson   1 2 3 4 5 6 7 8 9 10 11 12 13 14 15 16 17 18 19 20 21 22 23 24 25

COMPREHENSION SCORE

Put an X on the line above each lesson number to indicate your total correct answers and comprehension score for that lesson.

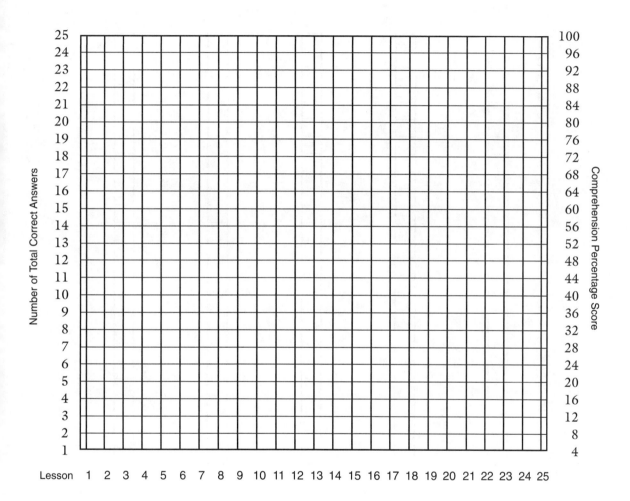

COMPREHENSION SKILLS PROFILE

Put an X in the box above each question type to indicate an incorrect reponse to any part of that question.

Lesson	Recognizing Words in Context	Distinguishing Fact from Opinion	Keeping Events in Order	Making Correct Inferences	Understanding Main Ideas
1					
2					
3					
4					
5					
6					
7					
8					
9					
10					
11					
12					
13					
14					
15					
16					
17					
18					
19					
20					
21					
22					
23					
24					
25					